John Vanderslice

Around the World

Sketches of Travel through many Lands and over many Seas

John Vanderslice

Around the World

Sketches of Travel through many Lands and over many Seas

ISBN/EAN: 9783337210113

Printed in Europe, USA, Canada, Australia, Japan

Cover: Foto ©Andreas Hilbeck / pixelio.de

More available books at **www.hansebooks.com**

AROUND THE WORLD.

SKETCHES OF TRAVEL

THROUGH MANY LANDS AND OVER MANY SEAS.

BY

JOHN VANDERSLICE.

PRINTED BY
J. B. LIPPINCOTT & CO.,
PHILADELPHIA.
1876.

Entered, according to Act of Congress, in the year 1876, by
JOHN VANDERSLICE,
In the Office of the Librarian of Congress at Washington.

TO

MY BELOVED AND VENERABLE WIFE,

WHO, BEYOND THE GATE OF FOURSCORE, GAVE ME HER
PARTING BLESSING AND WATCHED FOR MY RETURN
HOME; WHO NOW CALMLY AWAITS HER
SUMMONS TO THE BETTER COUNTRY.

PREFACE.

THE writer of the following pages has traveled in every State and Territory of the United States, Canada, Cuba, and the East, Great Britain and Ireland, France, Belgium, Holland, Germany, Italy, Egypt, Syria, Greece, Switzerland, Tyrol, Denmark, and Sweden; in whose company A. F. Shanafelt visited the ruins of Baalbec, roamed through the crooked street called "Straight" of Damascus, bathed in the Jordan near its source, and feasted at the summit of the Pyramids.

The journey of which the following pages contain a running account was undertaken by the writer mainly for the recovery of health, he having been paralyzed three times within ten years. The time devoted to traveling around the world was eight months, which may seem a short time when the great extent of land and sea is taken into account; but the facilities of travel are so great at the present day that more may now be accomplished in eight months than formerly in one or two years.

The actual traveling time in going round the world was eight months, distributed as follows:

From Philadelphia to Chicago, Omaha, Salt Lake, San Francisco, by rail, from the 29th day of September, 1874, ten days; from San Francisco on the 29th October, 1874, to Yokohama, twenty-six days on board; sail from Yokohama for the inland sea of Japan; arrive at Shanghai in eight days; sail to Hong Kong in time; go up to Canton, and then resume voyage from Hong Kong on the 10th December, so as to reach Singapore on the 18th; leave Singapore on 21st, and proceed through Straits of Malacca to Penang, and from thence to Point de Galle, Ceylon; we call at Madras, about midway between Point de Galle and Calcutta; we leave Madras for Calcutta January 29, 1875; at Benares, the holy city of the Hindoos; at Agra, Taj; leave Agra for Delhi; leave Delhi for Cawnpoor and Lucknow, and proceed to Allahabad; leave Allahabad for Jubbulpoor; leave Jubbulpoor for Bombay February 18, 1875; leave Bombay for Aden; leave Aden February 30 for Red

Sea and Suez; expect to arrive at Suez March 18; take railway for Cairo; leave Cairo for Alexandria; leave Alexandria and sail for Brindisi, and proceed for Naples; go to Rome March 30, 1875; from Rome to Pisa, to Spezzia, to Genoa, to Milan, to Turin, to Mont Cenis Tunnel, to Paris, to Calais, to London, to Liverpool, to sail across the ocean to New York, twelve days.

The natural order with the sun is the only practicable course, excepting at great expense of comfort and no little exposure of health and life.

The journey detailed in this volume was arranged with regard to these contingencies so accurately that the highest range of the thermometer occurring in its whole extent was in crossing our own continent at starting, and in landing at New York on the return, and yet in different parts of Asia that were visited the degree of heat during a large part of the year varies from one hundred degrees to one hundred and thirty degrees Fahrenheit in the shade. In India the thermometer often stands in summer at one hundred and twenty degrees and one hundred and thirty degrees during the day, and does not fall below one hundred degrees at night; but we neither saw frost during the entire year nor a higher degree than ninety to ninety-nine of the thermometer.

For the encouragement of future travelers around the world, it is well to state that the journey was made without accident of any kind, without the occurrence of serious illness to any of the party. More than once were we in perils on the land and on the sea, but, under the care of a kind and watchful Providence, we made the circuit of the earth, and returned to our home in safety, all the objects of our journey attained—health, pleasure, instruction, and a world of information concerning many lands and people gathered, which will be a life-long source of enjoyment.

AROUND THE WORLD.

BORN.

I, JOHN VANDERSLICE, JR., was born May 27, 1801, in Pikeland Township, Chester County, Pennsylvania.

MARRIED.

Was married October 20, 1825.

CHARLESTOWN, VIRGINIA.

In November, 1825, I started for Charlestown, Virginia. Stayed there and in the neighborhood three weeks. Returned by way of Harper's Ferry. Saw some of my old friends, among them Lewis Wormwag and Jesse Schofield, of Phœnixville.

FARMING.

In the spring of 1826 I commenced farming on a large place on thirds: the gentleman found all the stock and farming utensils. I started without a dollar, farmed four years, and then released.

DAYTON, OHIO.

May 28, 1828, I started for Dayton, Ohio, with Job Eldridge and wife; went as far as Wheeling, Virginia, in a carriage. I took the stage on the

National Pike for forty miles. This was then a first-class road. Then came to where the road was not macadamized, and went seven miles in the dark. The next morning took the stage back to Wheeling, then took a boat to Cincinnati, and from there to Dayton with my brother-in-law.

INDIANA.

Went from there to Indiana; bought a horse and returned to Dayton; remained there three weeks, and found company as far toward home as to Harrisburg. I then went into a speculation and made five hundred and thirteen dollars, clear of all expenses, after paying my fare, etc., in Halifax and Milton.

BUTCHERING.

I then carried on butchering for two years, made some money, and then bought a

FARM

in Pikeland, at Kimberton, for three thousand dollars. I kept the farm seven years, improved it very much, and sold it for eight thousand four hundred dollars, reserving about one acre, on which I built a house and barn; lived there about nine months, and sold it for two thousand dollars.

I then bought a tract of land in

PHŒNIXVILLE

for four thousand dollars. There was no building on this tract except my house, and none as late as 1840, except a few houses. Since that time I have been very busy. I have sold a great many lots to persons who wanted to buy at a fair price,—many for three thousand dollars for one-fifth part of an acre, and from that down to as low as two hundred dollars for the same quantity of land,—up to 1874.

LONDON.

May 15, 1851, I left Philadelphia in the steamer City of Glasgow for Liverpool, England. I had a very fine passage to Liverpool (eighteen days' sailing); stayed there four days, and started for London, stopping at all the towns on the way. Stayed in London ten days, and went to the World's Fair.

PARIS.

June 9, 1851, went to Paris, France; a splendid city. Spent ten days there, making many tours around the city. Left Paris by railroad for Chalons-sur-Saône, passing through many towns. There took a steamboat to Lyons, which is a beautiful city. There are seven hundred silk factories in Lyons. I embarked on the steamer Pekin for Avignon, on the Rhone. This is an old city of popery.

Here we took the cars for

MARSEILLES,

the chief port of the Mediterranean and steam-packet station for Italy. The population is over two hundred thousand. June 17, 1851, we embarked on the steamer Pharamond for Leghorn, which is a fine city.

PISA.

We visited the wonderful Leaning Tower of Pisa. It is worthy of all the fame it has acquired. It is about eighty feet in diameter and two hundred and fifty feet high, with marble stairs inside to the top. There is a fine view of the country from the top of this tower.

NAPLES.

Went back to Leghorn and took a steamer for Naples, which is a beautiful city, containing four hundred thousand inhabitants; went into the Catacombs, saw hundreds of rooms; walked up Mount Vesuvius and all over the top of it.

POMPEII.

Came back to Resina, then made our way to Pompeii. We entered the Nola Gate, saw the Amphitheatre, five hundred feet long and three hundred and fifty feet in width, capable of holding one hundred thousand persons. We went through every part of Pompeii, going out at another gate. We went to Herculaneum, visited the ruins of that city, then back to Naples, then toward the city of Rome, in a coach drawn by eight fine black horses. We passed a great many towns and through the Pontine Marshes, which are considered very dangerous. One is liable to fall asleep in passing these marshes, owing, as is supposed, to the impurity of the air.

TAVERNS.

We went to Three Taverns, where the great Apostle Paul had been. Here we took breakfast; then on to Rome.

ROME.

Rome has been one of the finest cities in the world. At one time it contained five millions of inhabitants, but now has only about one hundred and fifty thousand. It has dwindled down very much. It is still a very fine city, and has some of the greatest curiosities I ever saw. The Vatican and St. Peter's cover six acres of ground. Here you are never out of sight of cardinals, bishops, priests, monks, and nuns,—the whole number being over twenty-two thousand,—and the city has within it about twenty-four thousand beggars. I cannot name the curiosities to be seen in Rome. I went to see very many of them, and was much amused. The Pope resides here. I saw him more than a dozen times. We left Rome by stage for Civita Vecchia. This is a miserable poverty-stricken place. July 2, 1851, left this place in a steamship for Leghorn.

PISA.

We went from Leghorn to Pisa, thirty miles distant. I visited the Roman Cathedral, a very rich and magnificent building. The candlesticks in the church alone cost one hundred and forty thousand dollars. There are a great many splendid paintings and statues in the church, which is very handsomely carved. The ceiling is the most splendidly gilt that I ever beheld; it is about one hundred feet from the floor, and the galleries are far the finest I ever saw. The wonderful Leaning Tower of Pisa is worthy of all the fame it has acquired; it arrests the attention and awakens the admiration of every traveler; it is about eighty feet in diameter, two hundred and fifty feet high, and leans from the foundation to the top. On the inside is a staircase winding round and round to the top, built of marble. On the top of this tower is one of the finest views I ever beheld of the surrounding country, river, and sea. Near the burial-place is a baptismal font, which was built about one thousand five hundred years ago. It is a very large, high building, entirely round, and in the centre, where the water flows out and falls into the cistern which was used for baptizing in ancient times, there are four small cisterns at the top of the large one.

FLORENCE.

We next visited the city of Florence, which contains one hundred thousand inhabitants. It is strongly walled, as are most cities on the Continent, and is defended by several forts. Florence is a very fine city. I visited the studio of Mr. Powers, the American sculptor from Vermont, whose fame is already world-wide, and it will yet be felt that his Greek Slave and Fisher Boy are not his loftiest achievements.

July 6, 1851, left Florence in mail diligence, and, after leaving Porto San Gallo and passing the Triumphal Arch, we passed through one of the best, richest, and charming countries in the world, flanked with vines, orange-groves, olive-plantations, and fig-trees, until we gradually approached the pass of the

APENNINES;

and, as we ascended, looking back, I must say we had one of the most magnificent views I ever saw. We then came to Bologna, which contains seventy-five thousand inhabitants, and is a beautiful city. Left Bologna for Ferrara by way of Rovigo, and here passed out of the Papal States into Austria, crossing the river Po on a bridge of boats; arrived at Padua on the 9th of July, 1851. This is a fine city.

VENICE.

Here we took the cars for Venice, a city built on the sea. Venice is one of the most beautiful cities I have ever seen, although the streets are very narrow,—not more than from four to eight feet wide, and only one or two of the principal streets eight feet wide. The city is traversed in every direction by canals, which are thronged with gondolas. I visited the Ducal Palace and descended into the ancient dungeons, now tenantless.

I saw the ancient palace where thousands of persons had been beheaded. The blood remains on the wall near the guillotine about six inches thick. At the office the blood passed into the sea. I also ascended the bell-tower of St. Mark's, three hundred and thirty feet high, and had a magnificent view of the city, sea, etc.

VERONA.

July 10, 1851, left Venice for Verona, and passed through some of the finest, most beautiful, and richest country I ever saw. Left Verona in a diligence, passed some beautiful country and several old towns, traveled all night, and arrived in the city of Milan, about seventy-five miles from Verona, about eight o'clock A.M.

MILAN.

Milan, July 11, 1851.—This city is strongly walled, and contains one hundred and seventy-five thousand inhabitants. The most interesting object in Milan is its magnificent cathedral,—I think the most beautiful structure of the kind in the world, and only inferior in size to St. Peter's. It is a Gothic structure, built of the purest white marble, carved with a delicacy and lightness that is incredible, surmounted by a dome of the most delicate openwork and by innumerable spires. The elevated and delicate spire of the dome is surmounted by a colossal statue, and every spire is tipped with a statue rather larger than natural size.

There are an immense number of niches on every part of the extension of the building, all filled with statues, of which there are said to be no less than five thousand in and on the church. I ascended to the dome by four thousand six hundred and eighty steps. There is a forest of spires here. It is from the top of the dome that the most grand, magnificent view imaginable is obtained. At your feet lies the city, and around it a great number of beautiful villas; and farther on still are villages and towns in all directions, over the richest of countries, the plains of Lombardy, clothed with the most luxuriant vegetation, and intersected by innumerable rivers and canals that glitter in the sunshine.

Left Milan at twelve o'clock, July 12, 1851, for Lake Silvercords, via railroad to Lake Como, which we reached in two hours; thence taking the Swiss government diligence for Altorf, at the head of Lake Lucerne. We arrived at the town of Lugono and passed through her narrow streets, the widest not more than fifteen feet; thence to Bellinzona, a town of ten thousand inhabitants; followed the river to Mt. Gotthard.

AIROLO.

We reached Airolo, where the stage stopped at eight o'clock P.M., and stayed over-night, July 13, 1851. I left this pretty town about seven o'clock in the morning, in advance of the diligence, which did not start until nearly nine o'clock.

ALPS.

From Airolo I could see the main road for several miles, which, of course, runs zigzag up the Alps. I had to travel fifteen miles to reach St. Gotthard, but I could see a footpath that appeared to lead straight up the mountain. After ascending a considerable distance, I sat down to rest, finding the ascent too steep to travel. Here I overtook a fellow-traveler (German or Swiss). He informed me that he was from Reading, Pennsylvania, United States. I felt glad to meet a Pennsylvanian in St. Gotthard Alps. I kept in company with him to the summit. Stopped at St. Bernard to rest a little while; waited for the stage. When I overtook the stranger we were in among the snow, and only a third of the way up the mountain. After ascending farther, the water ran under the snow, which formed an arch across the channel or creek. The snow here was twenty feet deep, July 13, 1851. The creek is fifty-four yards wide; I crossed it on the bridge of snow. Here we had to take the oldest road, the new road not being open since the fall of snow. A little farther on is another place where the new road had just been opened through the snow, which is at least thirty feet deep, and stands perpendicular on each side of the road. I was now near the summit or convent of St. Bernard. Here the ground was covered with snow twenty feet deep, and all vegetation had ceased. Here is a little lake covered with ice from two to three feet in thickness. At the monastery are the dogs on the porch, great broad-chested, strong-limbed, of a dusky fawn color mixed with white spots, who never offer to bite. To these dogs many a poor benighted traveler owes his life from November to May. Here they changed horses, using only half the number to go down the mountain. We left the summit for Altorf, going down the mountain in zigzag at full speed. Almost one-third of the way down is a place they call the Devil's Bridge. Just before we came to this we passed through two tunnels. A little farther down there is a natural bridge across the river. It is composed of solid rock, and the water passes under it at a very rapid rate, and in many places has a descent of from five to six hundred feet.

ALTORF.

Here is the town of Altorf. It is impossible to estimate the quantity of ice on the Alps in Switzerland. I was told that independent of the glaciers in the Gresons there are fifteen hundred square miles of ice in the Alpine range from eighty to six hundred feet thick. Some glaciers, they say, have been stationary in the Alps from time immemorial. Altorf is situated at the head of Lake Lucerne. The town was erected in honor of William Tell, and stands on the spot where the Bailiff Gessler chained William Tell's son to a post in the market-place and compelled his father to shoot an apple off his son's head with a bow and arrow. William Tell succeeded in hitting the apple the first time, but when the tyrant asked him the reason of his having another arrow concealed in his dress, he replied, "To have killed you, had I killed my son." All this was done because William Tell would not bow to the hat of Bailiff Gessler. The offended Gessler had Tell seized, bound, and placed in the same boat with himself, resolved to carry him across the lake to his own castle and confine him. A frightful storm suddenly arose, and they were obliged to unbind the prisoner, who was celebrated for his skill as a mariner. He conducted them near to a ridge of rocks, jumping from the boat to a rock, at the same time pushing the boat back and sending it adrift. He escaped and concealed himself in a thicket, then waited for Gessler to pass on his way to his castle, and slew him. There is a small chapel erected upon the rock where William Tell leaped off the boat. I saw the chapel as I passed in the steamer. Altorf contains six thousand inhabitants.

LUCERNE.

Lucerne, July 14, 1851.—Stopped at the new and splendid Hotel Switzer Hoff, which contains about one hundred and fifty rooms and numerous saloons. Lucerne contains eight thousand inhabitants, a great many bridges of the finest kind, churches and cathedrals.

BASLE.

Left Lucerne July 15, 1851, for Basle, through Switzerland. Saw a great many cities and towns on the way to Basle. The present population of Basle is twenty-five thousand. It is built on both sides of the Rhine, and is the capital of the state.

STRASBURG.

Strasburg, July 16, 1851.—Strasburg contains seventy-five thousand inhabitants. The principal object of interest in Strasburg is the cathedral. The steeple was begun in the year 1276, and finished in 1439. The entire height of this building from the floor to the top of the spire is six hundred feet. The entire length is four hundred feet. I ascended to the top, and had one of the finest views I ever beheld. I could see all the city of Strasburg and many other large and flourishing cities. I could see Switzerland, France, and Germany, and up and down the Rhine for several miles I could see the steamboats plying in the river. The dome of St. Peter's, in Rome, is from six to seven feet lower. The great mechanical clock in Strasburg is in height about one hundred feet, and about thirty feet diameter and fifteen feet deep. Around me are many strangers waiting to see the working of the clock. As it strikes the hour of twelve or noon every eye is upon it. It now wants five minutes of twelve: now the clock has struck, and some of the people go out. The dial is thirty feet from the floor; on each side is a cherub or little boy with a mallet, and over the dial is a small bell; the cherub on the left strikes the first quarter, the one on the right the second quarter. Some thirty feet above the dial is a large niche, in which is a huge figure of Time, a bell in his left and a scythe in his right hand; in front stands a figure of a young man, with a mallet, who strikes the third quarter on the bell in the hand of Time, then turns and glides with a slow step around behind Time; then comes out an old man, with a mallet, and places himself in front of Father Time, and as the hour of twelve comes the old man raises his mallet and deliberately strikes twelve times on the bell, that echoes through the building and is heard all around the region of the church and city. Then the old man glides slowly behind Father Time. As soon as the old man has struck twelve and disappeared, another set of machinery is put in motion, some twenty feet higher. It is thus: there is a large cross with an image of Christ upon it; the instant twelve is struck, one of the Apostles walks out from behind, comes in front, turns, facing the cross, bows, and walks around to his place. As he does so, another comes out in front, turns, bows, and passes in. So twelve Apostles' figures, as large as life, walk around, bow, and pass on. As the last disappears, an enormous cock, perched on the pinnacle of the clock, slowly flaps his wings, stretches forth his neck, and crows three times, so loud as to be heard outside of the church for some distance, and so naturally as to be mistaken for a real cock; then all is silent as death. No wonder that this clock is the admiration of Europe! It was made in 1751.

BADEN-BADEN.

Left July 16, 1851, for Baden-Baden; passed through many towns and a fine country; stayed there four days. It is one of the finest bathing-places, perhaps, in Europe, and was one of the greatest gambling-places I ever saw, both for men and women. Left July 20, 1851, for Rastadt, which has a population of six thousand. Left for Carlsruhe, a very beautiful city; has twenty thousand inhabitants; they say it is one of the finest cities of the Rhine; the streets are very wide and the buildings very fine.

HEIDELBERG.

Left Carlsruhe for Heidelberg. It contains fourteen thousand inhabitants. Here is the largest hogshead in the world: it is thirty-three feet long, twenty-four feet high, and seventy-two feet in circumference. Went to Mannheim, a fine city on the Rhine, containing twenty-five thousand inhabitants.

FRANKFORT.

Went to Frankfort-on-the-Main. It contains sixty thousand inhabitants, and is the seat of the German Diet. It contains twenty-one open sewers, one hundred and fifteen fountains, and eighteen churches of different denominations. The chief part of the town is occupied by rich merchants, who live in elegant residences. A great many of the streets are very wide and handsome. The city contains about three thousand National Guards.

The most interesting sight is the Casino, an elegant building for amusement and refreshment. The first floor is devoted to reading, conversation, cards, and billiards. There are upwards of a hundred periodicals for the use of visitors. The ground-floor is devoted to refreshments and smoking. The Casino in Frankfort is conducted equal to any in Germany.

The garden of Baron Rothschild is situated on the right of Bockenheim road; admission is readily granted to respectable strangers. The museum contains a great many natural curiosities: minerals, antediluvian remains, mammalia, birds, and stuffed animals,—among them the hippopotamus, or river-horse—skeletons of fish, birds, animals, human skulls, reptiles, Egyptian mummies, Indian curiosities, eggs, and a great-coat made of sausage-skins, etc.

MAYENCE.

Mayence, formerly the residence of the first Elector of Germany, and more recently the chief place of a department of France, is now the most important town in the Grand Duchy of Hesse-Darmstadt; it is situated in the midst of the most beautiful and fertile country in Germany, opposite to the mouth of the Main, partly on the side of the hill and partly on the bank of the river Rhine. Its population is forty thousand, without including the garrison, which consists of twelve thousand Prussians and Austrians, making in Mayence a population of fifty-two thousand souls.

COBLENTZ.

Left Mayence in steamboat for Coblentz; passed down the river. Here is a town, Riebrich. After passing it, the hills on both sides of the river were covered with vineyards, the grape being extensively cultivated. Here is another town, situated at the mouth of the Nahi River; on the left is the mountain Rudesheim, and an old castle entirely surrounded by rocks, and standing on the very highest peaks. A little farther on are the ruins of another old castle, upon the highest rocks that can be seen. Here the river rushes with impetuosity toward a chain of black mountains, and afterwards suddenly toward the north, breaking against the rocks of the tower of Meuse, and a little farther down are the ruins of the tower last mentioned.

Still farther down is the place they call "The Devil's Ladder." The mountain is very high and the ascent very steep. Just below is the town of Lorch, in which it is said the first red wine was made in Germany. Still farther down the scenery is most magnificent. We are in sight of the city of Coblentz, which is on the Rhine and Moselle, at the confluence of the two rivers. Coblentz contains twenty thousand inhabitants, and is a very pretty city. There is a very strong fort on the high cliff of the rocks, from which I had a very extensive view of Coblentz and surrounding country. There are three thousand tons of cannon-balls in this fort. To Cologne. Passed some very pretty old towns and very handsome scenery. Bonn has a very beautiful appearance; it contains twenty thousand inhabitants, and has several very fine churches.

COLOGNE.

Cologne, July 21, 1851.—This city contains eighty thousand inhabitants. There are seventy thousand nine hundred and thirty-eight Catholics, six thousand four hundred and eighty Protestants, and seven hundred and eighty-four Jews. It is a walled city, and has nineteen gates of entry and thirty-four public squares. The cathedral is a great curiosity. It was commenced six hundred years ago, and is not yet finished; it is built in the form of a cross supported by a row of sixty-four pillars. There are altogether more than one hundred pillars. The four columns in the middle are each thirty feet in diameter. There are two towers or steeples five hundred feet high, unfinished. The bell weighs twenty-five thousand pounds. Cologne is one of the finest cities in Germany; the streets are wide and clean; the stores are all open on Sunday. It has more than two hundred churches of different denominations.

DUSSELDORF.

Dusseldorf, on the bank of the Rhine below Cologne, is low and the country very level. There are a great many towns along the Rhine; you are seldom out of sight of towers. Dusseldorf is the capital of the Grand Duchy of Berg, the seat of Parliament of the Rhenish provinces. It contains thirty thousand inhabitants; the streets are all at right angles and are wide. It is celebrated for picture-galleries, schools, and for the art of painting.

WESEL.

Left Dusseldorf for Wesel, which is well fortified by forts and a strong wall around the city, and contains thirteen thousand inhabitants. Here the Lippe falls into the Rhine. There is also a bridge of boats here across the Rhine. Left Wesel for Emmerich. Between these two places we passed ten very pretty towns on the banks of the Rhine. We are at Emmerich. Here on both sides of the Rhine for many miles the banks are covered with dwarf willows, which they use for making baskets.

We passed down the river Rhine. Here the river divides, the larger part of the stream being named the Waal. A little lower down it divides again, —one part, callel Yssel, taking a northern course. The Rhine proceeds east to Catwyk, and then divides again and forms two streams,—the largest taking the name of Leck. The Rhine, unlike most other rivers or streams, branches towards its mouth, and the part which retains the name of The Rhine is the largest of the many different branches.

ARNHEIM.

Arnheim is situated at the foot of a hill, and has twenty thousand inhabitants. The city contains many fine buildings for private residences, and has a great many fine gardens and public squares.

Here is Utrecht, which we are passing in the cars. Utrecht is said to be one of the most beautiful cities in Holland, and contains fifty thousand inhabitants. There is a tower in it which is four hundred and sixty-four feet high.

AMSTERDAM.

Amsterdam, July 21, 1851.—This city is of a semicircular form, and it is nine miles around it. It is surrounded by a canal eighty feet wide, and is entered by eight gates. It contains three hundred thousand inhabitants, about seventeen thousand of whom are said to be Jews. The whole city is built on piles driven into the mud. Under one house alone, it is said, there are fourteen thousand piles. As soon as Amstel River enters the city it is divided into two streams, from which there are canals branching off, communicating with each other and with the Y, and intersecting almost every street. These canals form ninety little islands, which are connected together by three hundred bridges,—some stone arched bridges and some draw-bridges.

I went to see the Royal Palace, which was built in 1750, and is said to be one of the noblest structures in Europe. It is situated in the centre of the Dam-Rak, and is two hundred feet square, exclusive of the tower. The principal hall is one hundred feet long, fifty feet wide, and the ceiling one hundred feet high. There are some of the most beautiful paintings in the palace that I ever saw. One alone was said to be worth ten thousand dollars. The palace is open every day to strangers, who have to write down their names when they enter, and pay the attendant what they please. I also visited the Royal Museum, the Post-Office, and the Barracks of St. Charles. Amsterdam is well supplied with all kinds of fish, sold very cheap,—a pair of large soles may be had for sixpence. I also visited the Corn Exchange, East India Warehouse, one-half of the building having sunk into the mud by the piles giving way, which causes the building to lean. I also went to see the dockyard and some charitable institutions, the Naval School, the Royal Institute of Science, and the Anatomical Theatre, with a museum containing anatomical preparations. Here are preserved the skeletons of felons sent for dissection. They are dressed in the clothes they wore when living, and are labeled with an account of their crime. I also went to see the Botanical Garden. The most exquisite taste is displayed in arranging and laying it out. Radius is one of the most beautiful spots in Holland. Attached to the establishment is an extensive menagerie, with well-arranged dens, containing a choice and rare collection of animals from all parts of the world. There is also a well-selected cabinet of natural history. The Roundel consists of one large room, well lighted, and a square court, planted with trees, from the branches of which the lamps are suspended.

The principal amusement of the place is dancing, and it is mostly crowded on Sunday evenings, as that is the day for amusement all over the Continent. In this are most of the Dutcheries. It is usual for the idle and dissolute to go to the Masin Spiel house or licensed brothel. The unfortunate girls are seated on both sides, or parading and dancing in the middle of the room, which is about one hundred feet long. At the entrance is a bar for the sale of refreshments, at which you are compelled to spend at least sixpence for admission. At the far end are the musicians in a gallery.

They say there are thirty thousand girls that follow that business in Amsterdam; they are licensed by the government, and entirely under the control of the police and physicians. They are not allowed to walk the streets after ten o'clock P.M. We traveled the city in every direction with gondolas, and some of the canals admit the largest vessels. The poor people wear wooden shoes, men and women. They wheel all kinds of vegetables, fruit, and country produce through the city on wheelbarrows. Some of them would haul nearly a cartload. This is one of the cleanest cities I have ever seen. Everybody looks clean; even the beggars in the streets are as clean as though every stitch of their clothing had come fresh from the washerwoman.

HAARLEM.

Left for Haarlem. The whole face of the country between Amsterdam and Haarlem is one continued meadow, intersected by ditches to drain off the water, without a tree or scarcely a bush in any direction, except what was planted in a straight line of more than five miles along the road and canal. About five miles from Haarlem is the Meer on the south and the lake or great water Ai on the north, containing an artificial isthmus. At this spot the relative heights of the two waters of the Ai and the Meer are nicely regulated by means of sluices and gauge-posts, marked into very nice and minute divisions; and the greatest attention is paid to the state of the waters at particular spots, the safety of Amsterdam and the adjacent country from inundation depending much on the management of these two inland seas. I saw some of the finest cattle feeding on those low, rich lands between Amsterdam and Haarlem that I have seen anywhere in Europe. Haarlem has a population of twenty-five thousand. It has one of the largest organs in the world,—consisting of eight thousand pipes and sixty-four stops. The largest pipes are thirty-two feet long and eighteen inches in diameter. To hear it played costs ten dollars,—eight dollars to the organist and two dollars to the bellows-blower. Not far from the church of St. Baron and in the great market-place is the house in which lived Laurent Coster, the inventor of printing. The first books which he printed are preserved in the town-house: they consist of two thin quartos, in black letter, on stout coarse paper. One of them contains a portion of Revelation; the paper is only printed on one side, which I saw and examined in the town-hall. In front of Coster's house stands his statue. He is represented in a consular robe, and his head is crowned with laurel; in his left hand is a piece of wood on which is engraved the alphabet, and in his right hand is a book. The statue, which is said to be a good likeness, is nine feet high, and the pedestal six feet high. Several inscriptions record the origin and removal of the statue, and there are some later verses by Van Zinter, his physician. On the east side Coster is represented walking in a wood and engraving characters on the bark of trees, and on the west side working in a printing-office. Haarlem is much celebrated for beautiful flowers: the tulip of the city is known in every part of Europe. In former times, it is said, one root was sold for ten thousand florins, and the aggregate sum procured by the sale of a hundred and twenty tulips was ninety thousand florins, or six thousand seven hundred and fifty pounds.

LEYDEN.

Left Haarlem for Leyden. This is a fine town, four and a half miles in circumference, situated on the Old Rhine, which alone carries its name to the sea, and which surrounds the town and supplies its numerous canals with water. Population, thirty-five thousand. Leyden has a University and a Botanical Garden, which is kept in the highest possible order,—the walks are beautiful and without a pebble,—covering an extent of seven acres, four of which have been added only a few years ago, laid out in good taste, for the reception of medicinal plants and for the use of medical students. Among the hot-house plants there is a date-palm with fruit upon it, which the gardener said had been there two hundred years. Nothing can exceed the cleanliness of Leyden in all its streets, inhabitants, and dwellings; the working and even the very poor class and beggars are clean. The canals running throughout the city have one hundred and fifty-five bridges with stone arches, besides many other bridges. The country from Haarlem to Leyden is beautiful meadow-land, except near the ocean, which is all sand-hills.

HAGUE.

Left Leyden for Hague. I went to see the principal places in Hague. I saw four beautiful palaces, the Museum, the Exchange, the King's Lottery House. I was in the House of Parliament, or German Diet, which was in session at the time. I could not understand any of their speeches more than a parcel of geese clattering. Few of the noble cities of Europe surpass it in beauty of streets, magnificence of palaces, or pleasantness of situation. The principal street is called Voorhout, but it may be rather called a street of palaces. Several rows of trees are in the centre, with gravel-walks; beneath them is a carriage-way on each side. There are canals running through the city in every direction.

ROTTERDAM.

Left Hague for Rotterdam (by railroad). This city is situated in the centre of South Holland. The population is seventy-five thousand. The city appears in size, beauty, and trade next to Amsterdam. The ground-plan of the city is a triangle.

Through the middle of most of the streets runs a straight canal, where the largest ships may land and unload at the doors of the warehouses; the streets are crossed by numerous draw-bridges; the houses are spacious and high, and in many of the streets they are really elegant, belonging chiefly to merchants and families occupying the upper stories. The hotels are good, and nothing can exceed the cleanliness of the houses and people. To every house in Rotterdam, and sometimes to every window of a house on the first floor, there is fixed a single or double looking-glass or reflector, by means of which a person in the room sitting before the window can see, by reflection, the whole length of the street—the passengers, the trees, the canal, and the shipping. Where two of these reflectors are placed at right angles, facing toward the window, a person within, directing the eye to the angle, will see the whole street both to the right and to the left. They say they are adopted for the amusement of the ladies. A stranger who has never seen a Dutch town is much amused. The combination of water, bridges, trees, and shipping in the heart of the city presents a novel and picturesque sight. The wooden shoes or sabots of the passengers are also novelties to the stranger. Left Rotterdam in the evening in a steam-packet for Antwerp, in Belgium.

ANTWERP.

Antwerp, July 24, 1851.—This ancient city is situated on the Scheldt River. It was once the chief mart of the Flemish and European commerce. In 1586 it contained two hundred and one thousand inhabitants, but it now contains only eighty thousand. The city is in the form of a semicircle, and is about seven miles in circumference. It has two hundred and twelve streets, eight churches, a custom-house, four canals, etc. There are some very fine cathedrals: the most noted one in Antwerp is five hundred feet long, two hundred and thirty feet wide, and two hundred and sixty feet high; the steeple is four hundred and sixty-six feet high. This cathedral has some fine paintings: one is the portrait of Mary Queen of Scots.

BRUSSELS.

Passed from Antwerp to Brussels, July 26, 1851. The first day I went to see the battle-ground of Waterloo; employed Monday (as guide), who was in the battle and belonged to the English army. He was to take us over the ground and show us the positions of both armies. He took us all over the battle-ground; but the corn and wheat again wave over the field that was so deeply dyed with blood, and almost all traces of the dreadful slaughter have disappeared, where seventy-six thousand brave followers were slain. There is a monument raised called the Lion's Mound, a vast accumulation of earth, one hundred fifty feet high. Beneath the mound there lie, indiscriminately heaped together, the bones of the slain, friends and foes. There is a round flight of stairs or steps leading to the top, where there is a huge lion standing on a pedestal ten feet high, from which an extensive view can be obtained of the surrounding country. Our guide showed us the barn, with a brick wall around it, which the English had possession of and which the French tried to take. They came down a narrow lane behind the barn, near the gate. The English had a fair fire on them, but they did not drive the French back until the dead and wounded lay six feet deep in the lane. Near the gate he also showed us a ravine, near which the English lines were formed, and to which he said thousands of wounded crawled and smothered one another. Near by he showed us a place where they had buried several thousand of the slain. The pit appeared to be about twenty-five feet wide and one hundred feet long, and was about one foot lower than the other soil around it. We returned to Brussels through the Black Forest, which is the thickest, heaviest, and best timber I ever saw grow. Brussels, the capital of Belgium, is beautifully situated on the river Senne, about fifty miles from the sea. Including its suburbs, it contains one hundred and seventy-four thousand six hundred and eighty inhabitants. The principal hotel is one of the best and most beautifully situated in Europe; it is in sight of the park, king's palace, etc., making it the most desirable stopping-place in Brussels. The expenses are about the same as at a first-class hotel in the United States. On the Place Royale stands a finely executed statue of Godfrey de Bouillon, by Simons. The principal portion of the city is built on the acclivity of a hill, and, viewed from the west, reminds the traveler of Genoa or Naples; the upper town contains the park, the royal court and government offices, the finest streets, squares, and hotels, and the residences of the richest classes. The lower town has a more crowded and mean appearance, and is the residence of the operative portion of the population, though it still abounds in fine old picturesque mansions, which were formerly occupied by the ancient nobles of Brabant.

PARIS.

From Brussels I continued my way to Paris, passing many fine cities. I stayed in Paris four days, then to the sea by railroad to Boulogne. Arrived at Boulogne (one hundred and seventy-five miles from Paris), which is a flourishing seaport town of great antiquity, and is divided into the high and low towns. The high town is connected with the low town by a street called La Grande Rue, and is surrounded by a rampart, which affords a fine prospect of the country in various directions. On the west the English coast may be seen in clear weather.

Boulogne contains twenty-five thousand inhabitants. It was where Bonaparte's army lay. It is also a great bathing place. Left Boulogne on 31st of July, 1851, at two o'clock A.M., in a steam-packet, by way of sea to the mouth of Thames River. Just as we entered the river, I could see one hundred and seventy-six sailing vessels and steamers going up and down the river.

LONDON.

Arrived at London Bridge at twelve o'clock on 31st day of July, 1851. Here we had our baggage examined by the custom-house officers, then took a cab and went to the Queen's Hotel. On the 1st of August, 1851, and for a few days after, I stopped at a private house in High Holborn Street, London. Spent two days in sight-seeing. Sunday, August 2, took passage at London Bridge for Greenwich Hospital, which is situated six miles below the bridge, on the Thames River. All the boats down and up the river were crowded with passengers. One starts every five minutes from London Bridge. Arrived at Greenwich at ten o'clock; went to see the hospital for old seamen and mariners, which is a very large building, or range of buildings. There are three thousand old, crippled seamen and mariners, deformed in every shape and manner, many of them confined to their rooms. Everything looks clean and healthy. I saw them take their tea, about six o'clock P.M. They had two very large rooms, where they had long tables set, and each man had a pint of tea, a small lump of butter, and a pound of bread for tea. It is said they sometimes give them meat. At the sound of a bell, all marched in in double file and took their seats in order as marked. After they were all seated and served, strangers were allowed to pass all through the building and look at them. There appear to be some very hard cases among them. All around the building are beautiful walks and flowers. There is also a gallery of paintings, which is very fine. There is a large park attached to the institution. In the centre rises a high mound, where there is a very pretty view. I could see London and many other towns, up and down the river, very plainly. I left at seven o'clock P.M. Took passage in omnibus back to London. Monday, August 3, 1851, went to see the General Post-Office, Bank of England, St. Paul's Church, the Lord Mayor's mansion, Charing Cross, Nelson's monument, all the bridges across the Thames, Whitechapel, and the Work-house. In the evening I visited the Vauxhall Garden. The performance was magnificent. August 5, 1851, went to the great London Exhibition. Was there all day. In the evening went to the Royal Zoological Gardens. Crossed the Blackfriar's Bridge. These gardens have very beautiful scenery and a large collection of wild beasts. There are all kinds of amusement. In the evening there is singing and a band of music of seventy-five players, the best I ever heard. It was Julien's Band. In the winding up was splendid fireworks. August 6, 1851, went to the Crystal Palace again. There were seventy-four thousand visitors during the day. August 7, 1851, I went to see the Duke of Northumberland's palace, went to Westminster Abbey, new House of Parliament, the National Gallery of Paintings, etc. August 8, 1851, I went to see the British Museum, where is the largest collection of antiquities I have ever seen. There is nothing belonging to an institution of that kind but what is there. They have a very large collection of mummies and old tombs. August 9, 1851, went through the city in almost every direction. Saw some very fine open squares, among others, Euston Square.

August 10, 1851, spent the morning at St. Paul's Church. It was so crowded that I could not get near enough to the preacher to hear one word he said. In the afternoon I took passage in steamboat and went up the river as far as Chelsea, to see the hospital for old soldiers. There were about five hundred soldiers here who had been wounded in the wars of England. This is a beautiful place on the river. Took omnibus back to London. August

11, 1851, left London; took passage in the cars for Liverpool; arrived at Liverpool the same day, when I met with Mr. Hallman, Doctor Amos Darlington, and Davis, who had traveled with me. Hallman and Amos were making ready to leave in the next steamer for America. Darlington, Davis and myself agreed to go through England, Scotland, Ireland, and Wales before leaving for America.

Left Liverpool August 13, 1851, in company with W. Darlington and Lewis Davis, proposing to take a tour through England. The first place we passed through of any considerable size and importance is Preston, which has a population of seventy thousand; then Lancaster, thirteen thousand inhabitants; next, Kendal, thirteen thousand; a rich and fertile country. After leaving Kendal, we left the cars and took passage in stage up Lake Windermere. The country is very hilly and mountainous. We passed a place which is called the highest inhabited ground in England. Here a great many sheep are fed. They are seen grazing on the hills in every direction. After passing a few miles farther, we passed down a lake two miles long. After we passed the lake the country became more level, and we soon arrived at a depot; there took the cars for Carlisle, and passed through a fine country, until we came to Gretna Green. This is the line between England and Scotland. From there to Dumfries, a town of fifteen thousand inhabitants. Went to see Burns's monument and the church he attended, and took a seat in the very pew in which he ofttimes sat. Saw the house he died in. Left Dumfries the 15th of August, 1851, for Cummer, in the cars; then for Ayr; then hired a private conveyance and went to see the house in which Burns was born. It is a small cottage. Next we went to see a monument that was erected in honor of him at a place he much frequented. Saw a very old church, perhaps the oldest in Scotland, with many old tombs.

AYR.

Went back to Ayr, and visited the place most frequented by Burns when on a spree. The place was named Tam o'Shanter and Souter Johnny, and there he used to meet company and sing and drink all night. The name is still on the house. Ayr appears to be a poor place, situated on the coast, and has ten thousand inhabitants.

PAISLEY.

Left Ayr for Paisley in the cars; passed through Irvine, a small town in a country broken and hilly.

Arrived at Paisley about ten o'clock A.M. Went to see several manufacturing establishments; visited the new school-house, which is nearly finished. A gentleman died lately, leaving thirty-five thousand pounds to it. It stands on very high ground, and commands a very fine view. The population of Paisley is fifty thousand. The chief manufactures are woolen and cotton goods. They make a great many broché Paisley shawls. Left Paisley about four o'clock P.M., and arrived at the city of Glasgow about five P.M. the same day. Passed through a valley, a rich and fertile country, where wheat, rye, oats, barley, potatoes, and vegetables are raised in abundance, it being one of the most fruitful parts of Scotland.

GLASGOW.

Glasgow, August 17, 1851.—Iron is said to be made cheaper here than elsewhere in the world. The ore is alloyed with a carbonaceous substance, which facilitates the process and reduces the cost of melting. Tall chimneys and black columns of smoke are abundant in the vicinity. The city contains three hundred thousand inhabitants, has a great deal of trade, and has risen rapidly from relative insignificance. A great many stately houses have recently been built, and it is rapidly improving toward the western side of the city. A dark-brown stone is the principal material used for building, and gives the city a substantial appearance. Near the buildings the stone is cut, and the joints are tight and uniform. Most of the town being new, has wide and straight streets. The old part of the town is the reverse. The town is built on both sides of the Clyde, which is crossed by five bridges, but seven-eighths of it lies on the north. Davis and I visited one of the poorest streets in the old part of the town. On entering it we came to a large Roman Catholic church. Saw them at mass. On entering the building, there was a man standing on each side of the door with a bowl in his hand. Every one who entered the door had to throw in at least a penny. There were a great many on the outside, on the large portico in front of the building, kneeling down. They appeared to be very poor, as they were all barefooted, and the women had no bonnets on their heads. They were as filthy and ragged as they well could be, many of them being not more than half clad. I asked one of them why they did not go inside of the church. She replied, they had no penny to put in the bowl, and were not permitted to enter. We saw hundreds of human beings, old and young, women and children, strolling the streets not more than half clad, barefooted, bareheaded, dirty, and ragged. There were a great many grog-shops, which these miserable creatures of both sexes were frequenting, drinking, and bloated to that extent that they could scarcely open their eyes. We went into one of these grog-shops, which was entered through a dark alley and by a rude flight of stone steps. It was in the second story, and the door was near the head of the steps. The main groggery was closed and bolted, a great crowd standing around it waiting for admittance. After waiting a considerable time,

I inquired of one of these people why they did not let us in. The reply was that they only admitted eight or ten at a time, and as soon as they were served they would pass out another way, and others would pass in. I inquired what they charged for a drink. They said a penny a drink. As the place was so disagreeable, Davis would not stay to go through, so we made our way back as we came. We went about one-fourth of a mile farther, and it was the same. I never before saw so much poverty and wretchedness in any place. Many other streets in Glasgow were the same, although near the centre of the ·city. All this part of the town is crowded with a miserable population, numbering not less than one hundred thousand; men and women, with children in their arms, and generally without shoes, stockings, bonnets, or sufficient clothing. Intemperance has many victims here, as throughout Scotland. There appears to be but little work for a great portion of the population of this city at this time.

At eleven we went to St. John's Church. Cotton and woolen goods are abundantly manufactured here. There are about one hundred cotton and woolen factories in the place, fifteen thousand power-looms and thirty-two thousand hand-looms. I went to see Tennant's soda factory, which is very large. It covers twelve acres, employs one thousand hands, and consumes seven hundred tons of coal daily. I saw the old Cathedral, the College, the Royal Exchange, the monument over John Knox, the reformer, and many other curiosities.

EDINBURGH.

Left Glasgow, in the cars, August 18, 1851, for Edinburgh. Passed through a beautiful, rich, and fertile country, and arrived at Edinburgh the same day, forty-eight miles. August 19, 1851. I knew this was a city of noble and beautiful structure. The old town was mainly built in a deep valley, running northward into the Frith of Forth, with the Royal Palace of Holyrood in its midst, the port of Leith on the Forth, a few miles northward, and the castle on a commanding crag overlooking the old town from the west. The Canongate and High Street lead up to the castle from the east, but its other sides are inaccessible; there being a deep valley on the north, while the south end of the town is separated by a deep valley northward, on which the new town of Edinburgh is built. The new town is one hundred and fifty feet above the old town, a mile and a half square, commanding a magnificent view of the old town, the port of Leith, the broad ocean-like Frith of Forth, and a finely cultivated country extending southward. I think it has more gardens and public squares than any other city of its size in the world. Its streets are broad and handsome, its houses built entirely of cut stone. I never saw so many good houses and so few indifferent ones in any place. Public monuments would seem to be the grand passion of Edinburgh. The most conspicuous are those of Lord Nelson, on Calton Hill; of Sir Walter Scott, on Prince's Street, which is the most magnificent I ever saw; also those of the pet Lord Melville, John Knox, and twenty or thirty others. There are several bridges across the rivers or gorges. These bridges are some of them seven hundred feet long and eighty feet high, and you look down from the roadway upon the red tiled roofs of eight-, ten-, twelve-, and fourteen-story houses in the old town, as many houses are fourteen and some sixteen stories high on the sides of hills. Every house in Edinburgh is built of stone; in the new part a fine quality of stone, handsomely cut, and of a brown or dark-gray color, being used. I was looking this afternoon at the Parliament House, which commands a fine view. Here I saw a piece of cannon called the Mons Meg, the largest ever known, banded with rough iron bands; the length was fifteen feet, the bore eighteen inches in diameter. I also saw in the castle the jewels that belonged to the kings of Scotland,—the crown, the sceptre, the sword of state, a silver rod or mace, etc. I also saw the house of John Knox, the principal churches, etc. I spent a considerable time in Holyrood Palace. Its top stairs are faded and rotten, its paintings are time-worn, its furniture has also felt the work of time. Its ball-room is now a lumber-room. The royal bed of Queen Mary stands just where she left it, with the same bedclothes and curtains around it, which are ready to fall to pieces. Her workstand and furniture in her dressing-room, her looking-glass, the first one that was ever made in Scotland (it is eight by ten inches), her candlesticks, etc., all remain.

Although Mary Queen of Scots has been dead three hundred years, these articles have been kept as relics; even the ivory miniature of the beautiful queen is still radiant with that loveliness which seems unearthly and prophetic of coming sorrows; and it were difficult to view without emotion the tapestry she worked, the furniture she brought over from France, the little room in which she sat at supper with Rizzio and three or four friends, when the assassin rushed in through a secret door, stabbed her ill-starred favorite, dragged him, bleeding, through her bedroom into an outer chamber, and there left him to die, his life's blood flowing from fifty-six wounds, leaving the traces of blood which are still visible upon the floor. The partition still stands which the queen caused to be erected to shut off the scene of this horrible tragedy from that portion of the reception-room which she was still obliged to occupy. I also saw James the First, King of England's, bed, just as he left it, with the furniture, etc., which has also been kept as a relic. Saw St. Giles's Church, the Cathedral, and the statue of Charles the Second. Edinburgh is entirely dependent on the courts, schools, and different colleges. There is but little manufacturing here. There are twenty-eight thousand more females than males in this city. Went to see Heriot's Hospital, probably the finest building in Scotland. Edinburgh is considered one of the most beautiful cities in Europe. The population is two hundred and fifty thousand souls. In the old part of the town there appears to be a great deal of poverty.

STIRLING CASTLE.

Left Edinburgh August 20, 1851. Went to see Stirling Castle, where I saw the ex-Queen of France, also viewing this old castle. She is the wife of Louis Philippe, the last King of France. Stirling has thirteen thousand inhabitants. Left Stirling same day, for Perth, in the cars.

PERTH.

Arrived at Perth at four o'clock P.M., August 21, 1851. Perth is said to be one of the handsomest and most ancient towns in Scotland, and contains twenty-five thousand inhabitants; it is situated on the west bank of the river Tay. It was the capital of Scotland before Edinburgh. Here, too, the Parliament and General Assembly was held. Here is a splendid bridge of ten arches, nine hundred feet long across the Tay; here the Reformation commenced, in consequence of a sermon preached by John Knox. The principal manufacturing is woolen and cotton.

STIRLING.

Left Perth, August 21, 1851, and went back to Stirling, then took a coach to Callander; passed through a beautiful country until we came to Callander. After passing that place, we passed along the lake called Venachoir, about five miles long; next we passed Achray Lake, about three miles long; next we came to Loch Katrine; there we took passage in a steamboat, and passed up to the head of the lake, which is ten miles long. After leaving the lake we took passage in the stage to Loch Lomond; we passed another small lake on the way, and through a very rough and mountainous country. The scenery is very beautiful; the mountains all look green with pasture, and there were one thousand or more sheep feeding on them. Arrived at Inversnaid, at the head of Loch Lomond, same day, August 22, 1851. Took passage from Inversnaid in a steamboat, and went down the lake as far as Ronardennan, then waited for a steamboat to come up the lake from Glasgow, and take passengers in here; back again to head of the lake, which was about eighteen miles. On the way up we passed a mountain called Ben Lomond, three thousand two hundred and ten feet high. At the head of the lake we took passage in the stage to

Oban, and passed through a very rough and mountainous country, but it was pretty well covered with grass, with thousands of sheep and cattle feeding on the hills. The whole country from Loch Katrine is very hilly and mountainous, and but very little timber. The pasture on these hills was generally very good. Arrived at Oban at five P.M.

OBAN.

Oban, August 23, 1851.—This appears to be a very old place; it is situated on the coast, and contains five thousand inhabitants. Left Oban 23d, in a steamboat, for Greenock; passed along the coast of Scotland, in among the islands, nearly all the way to the mouth of the Clyde. Arrived at Greenock the same day.

GREENOCK.

Greenock contains forty thousand inhabitants. The principal business is making machinery and ship-building. I went to see the tomb erected over the grave of Highland Mary, which contains a verse on it as follows:

> " My Mary dear, departed shade,
> Where is thy place of blissful rest?"

It was erected in 1842. Leaning on an urn above is an angel, neatly carved. The monument is about fifteen feet high and four feet square. It rained several times during the day, and the sea was very rough from Oban to Greenock. It has rained every day since I have been in Scotland (ten days).

BELFAST.

Left Greenock about eight o'clock P.M., for Belfast, Ireland. Took passage in steamship; fare, first cabin, ten shillings and sixpence. We arrived at Belfast about four o'clock A.M., after a very pleasant passage; the sea was calm and the night pleasant.

Belfast, Ireland, August 24, 1851.—Sunday morning, went to hear Dr. Cook, a Presbyterian minister, preach. It rained very heavily nearly all day. Monday, 25th, went to see Hinds & Co.'s linen factory, where there were upwards of a thousand hands employed, nearly all females, of all ages, from ten years upwards. The most of them looked well and were well clad, although some of the spinning-rooms, where they had a steamer for dampening the flax, were very warm and uncomfortable, and had a very disagreeable smell. I also went to see the linen hall, where they had a very large quantity of manufactured linen of different kinds. Belfast is a very pretty place, containing some fine open squares. The most of the people are Protestants. Next I visited Richardson & Co.'s linen store. From there I took passage in a jaunting-car, and went out to the bleaching works near Lisburn. I saw them putting the linen through the different processes for bleaching and finishing.

The finishing is done by putting it on large iron rollers, and then beating it with stampers.

LISBURN.

From there to Lisburn, a town of about five thousand inhabitants. From Lisburn I went back to Belfast, which has a population of one hundred thousand. Left Belfast August 25, 1851, in the cars for Ballymena; we passed through Antrim, a town of three thousand inhabitants, and through a beautiful country where they raised wheat, oats, and vegetables of all kinds in abundance.

BALLYMENA.

Ballymena, August 26, 1851.—I went out this morning to see the bleaching-green, which was a beautiful place; went out half a mile from the town to the poor-house, which was occupied at the time by two hundred paupers. I was told they had thirteen thousand in 1846 and 1847, the time of the famine in Ireland. It appeared to be well conducted, and everything clean and neat.

COLERAINE.

Left Ballymena for Coleraine; took passage in the stage; passed through a low, boggy marsh nearly all the way, where there is abundance of peat. Not one habitation in ten outside of the town is fit for human beings to live in; they are low, crammed hovels of stone, mud, and straw.

GIANT'S CAUSEWAY.

Coleraine, August 27, 1851.—Mr. Darlington,

AROUND THE WORLD. 55

Davis, Jones, Curtin, and myself took passage in jaunting-cars to the Giant's Causeway, by way of Port Rush; it is situated on the north coast of Ireland, and is an astonishing work of nature. It consists of vast numbers of perpendicular columns of basaltic rock from two to three hundred feet high; some three, some four, some five, some six, even seven, eight, nine cones, which were wedged in so as to fit every joint, as if it had been done by the most ingenious artist. It is certainly one of the greatest curiosities of nature I ever saw. There are also two caves at this place, one of them being three hundred feet long and sixty feet high. I went into it from the coast side; the other is five hundred feet long and sixty feet high. The one I went into is in the shape of a T. The rocks along the coast are very bold, and are formed of limestone and flint. After leaving the Causeway, went back to Coleraine by way of Bush Mills, where, it is said, they make the best whisky in Ireland.

COLERAINE.

Coleraine has a population of thirteen thousand. It is situated on the banks of the river Bann, which empties into the sea five miles below. Then to Newtown-Limavaddy; then to Londonderry; then to Lifford and Strabane; then to Ballybofey; then to Omagh; then to Portadown; then to Armagh; then to Newry and Warrenpoint; then to Dudnalk; then to Castle Bellingham; then to Drogheda; then to Dublin, the capital of Ireland; then to Naas; then to Rosera; then to Maryborough; then to Templemore; then to Thurles; then to Charleville; then to Mallow; then took the stage for the Lakes of Killarney, by way of Millstreet and Killarney; went through the lake in every direction we could, and back to Killarney Hotel. Next day went back to Mallow; then to Cork; then to Cloyne, to Queenstown, or Cove of Cork; then back to Cork, Mallow, and Dublin, by Kingstown; then took a steamer and crossed the Channel to Wales; then took the cars to the Tubular Bridge, which spans an arm of the sea, and is one of the greatest bridges I ever saw. From there to the Bangor slate quarries, several hundred feet deep; then to Chester; then to Liverpool. Went back to London. Went to see the glass factories, and down the Thames River and back to London.

LIVERPOOL.

From there we went to Liverpool, and took passage in the City of Manchester to Philadelphia. Arrived at Philadelphia in eighteen days, by a nice passage. Then home to Phœnixville. Away from home about seven months in 1851.

CHICAGO.

In 1855 I started for Chicago; went to Davenport; went across Iowa to Fort Des Moines; went through the State to Council Bluffs; went across the Missouri River to Omaha: not more than five or six houses built in that city; then back. Took a boat down the Missouri River to St. Louis, stopping at all the towns on the river.

ST. LOUIS.

I stayed at St. Louis about two weeks, and then started up the river to Davenport. Then I bought about eighteen hundred acres of land at Government prices ($1.25 per acre). I kept it two years, and then commenced selling it. I made out very well with the land. I still have one farm. I was offered twelve dollars per acre this spring (1874).

NEW ORLEANS.

I started at Davenport to go down the Mississippi River to New Orleans; stayed there about three weeks.

CUBA.

I then took passage on the Black Eagle, the 25th day of December, 1855, for Cuba. It was a very rough passage; the captain said it was the roughest passage he ever had. We came to Havana after sundown, and they would not let us in. So we took to the sea, and got in the next day about ten o'clock A.M. We had some difficulty in getting in on account of passports. I stayed in Cuba one winter. I traveled some eight hundred miles on the island. There was a man went with us from New Orleans who had the consumption. He traveled with us on the island, came back to

Havana, and died. He came into my room, and said he could not get his breath. I got up, and wanted him to lie down; he would not. I went to bed again. He breathed very hard. I got up again, and insisted on him to take the bed. He took the bed and laid down, and presently I went out for the family. They came in, and he died. We buried him in a vault. It cost some money to bury him. Two days after he was buried, we started for America. We landed at Key West, in Florida. We sailed for Charleston; stayed there ten days. I went from there to Mobile; stopped at all the towns on the road.

MOBILE.

Mobile is a very fine city; contains two hundred thousand inhabitants.

WASHINGTON.

I left Mobile for Washington, D. C. Stayed there ten days. From there home to Phœnixville. Stayed six months in 1855 and 1856.

M'GREGOR'S.

In 1858 I made a trip to Chicago; stayed there four days; went to McGregor's; from there to where my land was situated; sold a good quantity of it at a fair price. Away from home three months; back to Phœnixville.

In 1859 I made another trip to Chicago; stayed two days; went to McGregor's, on the Mississippi River; from there to many parts of the State of

Iowa. I sold several hundred acres of land at good price. Came back to the river.

ST. PAUL.

Went up the river to St. Paul; from there to Minneapolis; saw the Falls of St. Anthony, a great affair. I went to see many cities and towns in the State. Went back to St. Paul; down the river to La Crosse, to Madison, to Milwaukee; then across Lake Michigan to Grand Haven; very rough passage; behind time. The captain said it was very rough; laid over eight hours.

DETROIT.

From there to Detroit. Crossed the channel to Canada; went to London, then to Toronto, a very fine city, then to Montreal, a beautiful city, building a tubular bridge over the St. Lawrence; then down the river to Lake St. Peter, and to many places where they had thousands of thousands of feet of lumber stowed away.

QUEBEC.

Quebec is a fine city. Has a fort from which the officers told me they could hit a vessel down the St. Lawrence five miles. The officers took me through every part of the fort. To Lancaster; to the White Mountains, in New Hampshire.

PORTLAND.

From there to Portland, Maine, to Concord, to Boston, one of the finest cities, perhaps, almost in the world, to Providence, a fine city, to Hartford, to New Haven, to New York, to Philadelphia, to Phœnixville. Away five months from home, 1859.

ARMY.

"July 5, 1861.

"Pass Mr. Vanderslice three days over the bridge and within the lines (Potomac).

"By order of General Mansfield, commanding.

" "DRAKE DE KEY,

"*Aid-de-Camp.*"

July 14, 1861, went to Fort Monroe.

"Pass Mr. Vanderslice to Camp Hamilton and within the fort for two days.

"Captain P. A. DUNS,

"*Provost-Marshal.*"

"WASHINGTON, July 29, 1861.

"Pass John Vanderslice over the bridge and within the lines (Potomac) one day.

"By order of General Mansfield, commanding.

"DRAKE DE KEY,

"*Aid-de-Camp.*"

"WASHINGTON, D. C., January 31, 1863.

"The bearer, J. Vanderslice, and daughter, have permission to visit the company of the Potomac for the purpose of sick husband Doct.

"By order of Secretary of War.

"M. OMER."

"HEADQUARTERS OF FIRST DIVISION, DEPARTMENT OF SUSQUE-
HANNA, July 3, 1863.
" Guards,—Pass J. Vanderslice through the lines
to Gettysburg.
" General W. L. SMITH.
" R. H. LAMBORN,
" *Captain and Aid-de-Camp.*"

ARMY.

July 1, 1863, went out with the army from Phœ-nixville, Pennsylvania, to Harrisburg; stayed there a few days; enlisted in the army until Lee was driven out of Pennsylvania and Maryland, and went to Gettysburg after the road was opened; stayed but a few hours, when Lee's army crossed the Potomac and came up and had a battle. We started back in the cars; put out all the lights. Lee's cavalry went to burn a bridge, but we got over before it was burned; went to Carlisle, and stationed there two nights. Lee's cavalry came in sight. This night we packed up and went below Carlisle, then encamped. I got a pass to go to Harrisburg. The army soon came to the Susquehanna; stayed a few days, when we heard that Lee's army had burned the barracks and a good part of Carlisle. We soon marched to Carlisle, and from there toward Gettysburg; lay on the mountain, expecting the rebs to come back that way. Laid there until after the battle was over.

6*

GETTYSBURG.

I got a pass, with J. H. Sultzen, to visit Gettysburg and see the fatal result of the battle. Saw hundreds of soldiers on the battle-field in different places; was upon Round Top. Stayed in Gettysburg three days, then went to the army. Went through different towns to Carlisle, where the army laid. Had a small battle there. We saw the rebels about eight hundred yards off. The soldiers, many of them, fired at them. I fired also. There was a bullet came over us and struck a tree, where there was a boy standing. The bullet struck just above his head. He scampered away very quick. That night they decamped and went to Williamsport. Many of them crossed over the Potomac, and many went to Falling Waters before they could cross. The cavalry overtook them and slew hundreds of them. I went down the river Potomac. At Williamsport the rebels on the other side fired over to us, and we made off, and, going up the street, a ball passed over our heads and struck a house just before us. Here at Williamsport I got discharged from the army, and went to Falling Waters, where we saw hundreds of men lying dead over the field and thousands of muskets and rifles lying in the field. Went back to Baltimore; from there to Philadelphia, and home to Phœnixville. Away from home fifty-three days.

"HEADQUARTERS, LIGHT DIVISION, WAYNESBURG.
"July 11, 1863.
"Guards of Patrol,—Pass J. S. Seltzler and John Vanderslice through our lines.
"By order of KILLKED and SEIKEL.
"CAPTAIN MANSFIELD."

ARMY.

"FORT WASHINGTON, PROVOST-MARSHAL'S OFFICE,
"BRIDGEPORT, COLUMBIA COUNTY, July 18, 1863.
"Guards at the bridge will pass John Vanderslice to Harrisburg and return.
"By order of CAPTAIN WM. B. MANN,
"*Provost-Marshal.*"

"HEADQUARTERS, PROVOST-MARSHAL'S OFFICE.
"July 19, 1863.
"Picket Patrols,—Pass John Vanderslice through the pass to the Pennsylvania Reserves and return.
"R. H. HOLMES."

KUSSERT.

October 1, 1863.—In Phœnixville I went into a speculation, in the Kussert Farm Oil Company. John Vanderslice bought four hundred and fifty shares, Greene County, Pennsylvania, in the capital stock of Kansas Oil Company, the 27th day of October, 1865. J. C. Reeves, Secretary; William C. Baker, President. I also went into more Kussert Oil Farm Company, Greene County, Pennsylvania: four hundred shares, at five dollars per share. J. Vanderslice, October 30, 1865. J. C. Reeves, Secretary; William C. Baker, President. I also went into more Kussert Oil Company, Greene County, Pennsylvania: four hundred shares, at five dollars per share. John Vanderslice, October 30, 1865. J. C. Reeves, Secretary; William C. Baker, President. I also went into more Kussert Oil Company, Greene County, Pennsylvania: four hundred shares, at five dollars per share. J. Vanderslice, November 4, 1865. J. C. Reeves, Secretary; W. C. Baker, President. I also went into another speculation in the Golden Gate of Montana Mining Company. J. Vanderslice bought one hundred and fifty-six shares, at ten dollars per share, November 24, 1865. Joseph Morse, Secretary; J. R. Weeks, President. Golden Gate of Montana Mining Company, J. Vanderslice bought one hundred and fifty-seven shares, at ten dollars per share, November 30, 1865. Joseph Morse, Secretary, J. R. Weeks, President. Golden Gate of Montana Mining Company, J. Vanderslice bought one hundred shares, at ten dollars per share, July 9, 1866. Joseph Morse, Secretary; J. R. Weeks, President. I also bought several other shares at Oil City; paid the money for the shares. After all, the stock is not worth one cent, and all I mentioned above is all lost. July 20, 1868.

WASHINGTON.

October 11, 1868.—Left Phœnixville through Philadelphia and Baltimore for Washington, D. C.

From there took a boat, went down the Potomac and cars to Fredericksburg, Virginia, to Richmond, the capital of Virginia, a fine city, to Scottsville, to Marysville, to Halifax, to Yanceyville, to Greensborough, to Lexington, to Salisbury, where the rebels punished our soldiers, to Concord, to Charlotte, to Yorkville, to Unionville, to Lawrenceville, to Edgefield, to Augusta, a fine city, to Jacksonboro', to Savannah,—a fine city; streets laid out very finely and many public buildings,—to Charleston, South Carolina.

FORT SUMTER.

Fort Sumter, all in ruins; then to Charleston,— stayed there five days. Then to Summersville; then to Branchville, to Blackville, to Aiken,—one of the finest places in South Carolina for the benefit of a person's health if sick,—to Augusta, in Georgia, to Crawford, to Covington, to Jackson, to Macon,—a fine city; fine buildings and squares, —to Howardsville, to Darien, to Brunswick, St. Simon's Sound, on the Atlantic Ocean,—stayed there eight days,—to Fernandina, to St. John's River.

JACKSONVILLE.

Jacksonville, Alabama, up the river to Mandurin, to Picolata, opposite to St. Augustine, to Pilatka. Opposite, across the river, is an orange grove, with thousands of trees, orange and lemon, in full bearing, thousands of them; the proprietor gave me plenty of both kinds; and up the river, passing many towns; then back to Jacksonville,—stayed ten days; then to Alligator, to Cedar Keys, on the Gulf of Mexico,—stayed five days; then back to San Pedro; then to

TALLAHASSEE,

the capital of Florida, to Quincy, to Bairnbridge, to Hamburg, to Columbus,—a fine city; fine buildings and many squares,—to Tuskegee, to Montgomery, the capital of Alabama,—a beautiful city, to

PENSACOLA,

on the Gulf of Mexico; then back by railroad and steamer until we came to Mobile. There the yellow fever was very bad; two-thirds of the inhabitants left the town,— stayed four days, then to

NEW ORLEANS,

—stayed ten days. Left New Orleans for Galveston by rail and water.

GALVESTON.

Galveston is a fine city,—splendid buildings. Went from Galveston by railway through Texas; passed many cities and towns; most excellent land, and some well improved. Went back to Galveston; then to New Orleans by steamer and railroad,—stayed at New Orleans five days; then up the Mississippi River to Red River, to Baton Rouge, to Port Hudson, Bayou Sara; then up

Red River to Alexandria, to Carnfet, to Port Caddo, to Shrevesport; then up the little Red River to Texas,—a beautiful country; then back the Red River to Mississippi; then to Natchez, to Rodney, to Vicksburg, to Princeton, to Bolivar, to Mark, Arkansas River; then to Peyton, then to Memphis, then to Bolivar, then Savannah, then Lawrenceburg, then Columbia, then Franklin, then Nashville, the capital of Tennessee,—a first-rate city; then Greenville, Kentucky; then Louisville, a fine city; then through Illinois to St. Louis,—a fine city; from there to Alton, from there to Springfield, where we saw Lincoln's monument; then to Bloomington, to Chicago; from there to Sandusky; then to Pittsburg; then to Philadelphia; then Phœnixville. Away from home four and a half months, in 1868 and 1869.

CALIFORNIA.

I started for California, May, 1871. I went to St. Louis; went down to the Iron Mountain, where they quarry out thousands of tons of ore; saw the blast-furnaces, went over the railroad to San Francisco; about twenty-one days going out; stopped at all the places worth seeing. I traveled all over the State, down the valleys and up the valleys, to the Geyser, up one valley and down the other over Hog's Back, four miles of road just the width of the wagon; not more than eighteen inches each side of the road, and if the wagon went down it would fall one thousand feet, five hundred feet, three hundred feet, etc. Got into a splendid valley back of San Francisco; from San Francisco to Sacramento City, Marysville, Reading, through Oregon to Portland, over one of the roughest roads I ever saw; from there to Washington, to Olympia, to see where the great railroads end; down the Olympia to Vancouver's Island, also to British Columbia, where there are gold mines; came back to the Columbia River, sailed up in a steamboat, passed three falls, saw the Indians fishing for salmon; came back to Portland; then took a steamer back to San Francisco; stayed there one week; then took a steamship down the Pacific Ocean to Panama; stopped at many places on the coast or towns; then by Panama Railroad to Aspinwall; then by steamship to New York, passing many islands; on the passage thirty-one days; then to Philadelphia; then to Phœnixville. Away nearly seven months in 1871. I will try and give you an account of my travels through Europe.

GLASGOW.

I left New York 15th day of June, 1873. We landed at Glasgow on the 25th day of June, after a fine passage. The chief portion of Glasgow lies on the north bank of the Clyde, which is crossed by five bridges, and lined with magnificent quays. Glasgow is noted for the quantity and purity of its supply of fresh water, brought through tunnels, aqueducts, and reservoirs from Cussie, Loch Katrine, a distance of thirty-four miles; the supply being equal to twenty-four million gallons daily. The Great Western Cooking Depot, the object of which is to provide cheap food for the working classes; this depot, with its numerous branches, supplies a good, substantial breakfast for threepence, and dinner, consisting of soup, meat, potatoes, and pudding, for fourpence halfpenny. Here is a city importing food from us and supplying it to its workmen in good condition,—good breakfasts and dinners, fifteen cents per day.

The first and most prominent object to be seen in Glasgow is the Cathedral, which, I think, ranks next to Westminster in the Kingdom, and is certainly equal to the far-famed Salisbury Cathedral for purity of style. The most conspicuous monument is that erected to the memory of John Knox, the great reformer. It is situated on the highest elevation of the grounds, and the statue is placed on the top of a fine Doric column; and he whom Scotland delights to honor looks down upon the tombs of many of the great who are buried around. Glasgow possesses a university of high repute as a seat of learning. The Royal Exchange, situated in the centre of Exchange Square, is, perhaps, the finest building in Glasgow. The Royal Bank, which is situated behind the Exchange Square, is also a very beautiful building. Visitors are generally admitted into Bothwell Castle on Tuesdays and Fridays; the building is an oblong quadrangle, built in Norman style of architecture, two hundred and thirty-four feet long and one hundred feet wide; the walls are thirteen feet thick and sixty feet high; there is an immense circular dungeon, called Wallace's Beef Barrel, twenty-five feet deep by twelve wide; the ruins, which are covered with ivy and beautiful flowers, was once the residence of the haughty chieftain, Sir Andrew Murray, who was the first to join the hero Wallace, and the last to leave him. Glasgow is the commercial city of Scotland, and is the most populous. It contains five hundred thousand inhabitants. The principal hotel is Meclen's, in St. Vincent Street. Stayed there two days, and from there to Edinburgh; time, two hours, via Lennox Town, Falkirk, and Linlithgow. Edinburgh is the capital of Scotland, and is situated on two ridges of hills, within two miles of the Frith of Forth, and contains two hundred thousand inhabitants.

EDINBURGH.

Edinburgh, for its size, is one of the most imposing, interesting, and magnificent cities in Europe. Through its centre a deep, wild, and rocky ravine extends, dividing the city into the old and new towns. On Prince's Street most of the hotels are located. Here is Philip Cockburn's Temperance Hotel; stayed there three days. Sir Walter Scott's monument is two hundred feet high, and has two hundred and eighty-seven steps leading to the top of the gallery. St. Giles' Cathedral is magnificent in its appearance. The University of Edinburgh, founded by James VI., is a fine educational establishment, having a library containing one hundred thousand volumes. The next important memorial of Scotland's ancient greatness is the remains of Holyrood; it was a magnificent building in former days. Both palace and abbey are open to the public every day, except Sundays. The palace was the ancient residence of Scottish royalty. The most interesting rooms in the palace are those last occupied by the unfortunate Mary; her bed-chamber remains in the same state as when she left it, and the cabinet where her secretary and favorite Rizzio was murdered is shown, with marks of his blood still upon the floor. The roofless choir is shown where once stood the altar before which the beautiful Mary, the next nearest heir to the English crown, and Henry Darnley were united. In the picture-gallery are some frightfully-executed portraits of over one hundred of Scotland's kings, evidently painted by the same hand and from imagination. We now leave Edinburgh for Liverpool, passing many towns on the way.

LIVERPOOL.

Liverpool is situated on the east side of the

river Mersey, near its mouth, and extends three miles in length along its banks. It is the second city in the Kingdom, and contains about six hundred thousand inhabitants. Liverpool is noted for the magnificence of its docks, which are constructed on the most stupendous scale, covering, with the dry docks, two hundred acres, fifteen miles of quays. Nearly one-third of its trade is with the United States. The cotton which formerly arrived here annually amounted to two million five hundred thousand bales. The Zoological Gardens cover ten acres of ground, and are tastefully arranged. We visited more than one thousand places in Liverpool; stayed there two days. After leaving Liverpool, we started for Manchester, then to London.

LONDON.

London is the metropolis of the United Kingdom of Great Britain and Ireland, and the most wealthy city in the world. Population in 1873, almost three million two hundred thousand, about one million increase in twenty-two years. The present increase is about forty-four thousand per annum, or a birth about every four minutes. The city covers an extent of one hundred and forty square miles: fourteen miles long and ten broad; three hundred and sixty thousand houses are occupied by the population of the city; the cost of food is supposed to be eight hundred thousand dollars per day; and although the climate of London is by no means pleasant, its sanitary advantages over other capitals are remarkable. According to the statistics, out of every thousand inhabitants twenty-four die annually in London, while in Berlin and Paris twenty-eight, and St. Petersburg forty-one, out of the same number of population.

The streets are mostly wide, clean, and well paved; the houses plain and substantial; the architecture of the club and public buildings is substantial and elegant. The Tower of London is supposed to have been commenced by Julius Cæsar. This celebrated fortress is situated at the eastern extremity of the city, and is separated from the thickly-populated portion of the city by what is called Tower Hill. It covers twelve acres of ground, and is surrounded by a moat, which since 1843 has been used as a garden. On the river-side is an entrance called the Traitor's Gate, through which persons of state were conveyed in boats after their trial. Within the famous structure are numerous buildings, including the Armory, Jewel-House, White Tower, St. Peter's Tower, Bloody Tower, where Richard III. murdered his nephew, the tower where the Duke of Clarence was drowned in a butt of Malmsey wine, the Brick Tower in which Lady Jane Grey was confined, the Beauchamp Tower, the prison of Anne Boleyn, and numerous other buildings.

In addition to the tower being originally used as a fortress, it was the residence of the monarchs of England down to the time of Elizabeth, and a prison for state criminals, and numerous are the kings, queens, warriors, and statesmen who have not only been imprisoned, but murdered within the walls. The histories of Lady Jane Grey, Catharine Howard, Anne Boleyn, Sir Walter Raleigh, Sir Thomas More, William Wallace, and King John of France, do they not live in the remembrance of every reader of history?

In addition to the historic points of interest which I visited, I will be conducted through the Armories and Jewel-House, and, after waiting until a party is collected, which is done every half-hour, a warden dressed as a yeoman of the time of Henry VIII. will show me through the Armory, and then intrust me to the care of a female, who will describe the use and value of the regalia in the Jewel-House.

The Bank of England is the most extensive banking institution in the world; is situated north of the Royal Exchange. About one thousand four hundred clerks are constantly employed here, at salaries ranging from three hundred to six thousand dollars per annum. The building is rather low, and peculiar in appearance. With the courts, it includes an area of about eight acres. Many of the offices are open to visitors, but the private ones can only be visited by an order from the directors. The most interesting apartments are the bullion-office, weighing-office, treasury, and the apartment where the bank-notes are printed. Here is a steam-engine, which moves printing-machines, plate-presses, etc., and from its beautiful movement forms a very interesting sight. The management of the bank is invested in a governor, deputy-governor, and twenty-four directors. I noticed especially the remarkable weighing machine.

The General Post-Office, St. Martin's-le-Grand, is a spacious building, in Ionic style, with lofty central porticoes. The establishment employs more than two thousand clerks, carriers, etc. Into the different parts of the United Kingdom about six hundred millions of letters are delivered annually, one hundred and fifty millions in London alone, in addition to seventy-four million newspapers and five million books and parcels. The annual postage revenue amounts to seventeen million dollars.

The principal bridges of London are, first, the London Bridge, built of granite, between 1825 and 1831. It cost ten million dollars; it is nine hundred feet long and fifty-four feet wide. The lamp-posts are made of cannon taken during the Peninsular war. One hundred thousand people pass over this bridge every day; it is the longest bridge, or that nearest the sea.

The next bridge in order is the Southeastern Railway Bridge, by which Charing Cross is connected with Canon Street terminus. Blackfriars' Bridge, built between 1864 and 1869, of iron, one thousand two hundred and seventy feet long and seventy-five wide. Dover Bridge, for railroads. Hungerford Bridge, built of iron, in 1863, for Charing Cross railway station; foot passengers alone cross. Waterloo Bridge is a splendid specimen of substantial architecture; it was built by a private company, between 1811 and 1816; it is one thousand three hundred feet long and forty-three feet wide; the toll is one cent, which amounts to fifty thousand dollars annually. Westminster Bridge is the most elegant of all the London bridges. It was finished in 1862; it is constructed of iron on stone piers, is one thousand one hundred and sixty feet long and eighty-five wide, probably the widest in the world. From this bridge a most excellent view can be had of the river front of the beautiful House of Parliament. There is also Lambeth Bridge, Vauxhall, Pimlico Railway Bridge, and Pimlico Suspension Bridge. The Thames Tunnel, beneath the bed of the Thames, was originally intended for carriages; it was commenced in 1825, finished and opened to the public in 1843; Brunel was the architect; its total cost was nearly two million five hundred thousand dollars; it is now used as a railway, connecting the Great Eastern and North London Railways.

The principal docks of London are the St. Catharine's Docks, situated near the Tower, covering an area of twenty-four acres, of which eleven are water. The cost of this immense undertaking was over eight million dollars; twelve hundred houses were pulled down to make room for them. London Docks cover ninety acres, thirty-four of which are water, the rest being warehouses and vaults, where there are thousands and thousands of barrels of wine. There are also the East India Docks, the West India Docks, Surrey Docks, Millwell Docks, etc. Many other places of interest were visited. Stayed in London five days, then left for Paris.

PARIS.

The inhabitants of Paris have long considered themselves at the head of European civilization, and, if such an eminence can be obtained by mere external polish, they deserve it. In matters of dress and fashion the lead is conceded to them by a kind of universal consent, and, though their manners have suffered considerably by the stormy periods through which they have passed, their native politeness has not been lost. None succeed better, not only in practicing the agreeable arts of life, but in observing the outward decencies of society. Beneath this pleasing surface, however, a strong and polluted current is perpetually running, and there is no part of the world where the more substantial virtues are more rare and where so much dissoluteness exists within such narrow limits.

The order of the Legion of Honor was established in 1802. The emperor was then grand master. It has now over fifty-five thousand members. Nearly every crowned head in Europe is a member of it. Attached to this order is the Maisons Imperiales, an establishment devoted to the instruction of sisters, daughters, and nieces of the members of the order. It was established by Napoleon I. Four hundred pupils receive here a finished education at the expense of the government. They all dress in black, with black bonnets, and are subject to the most rigid discipline. To obtain permission to visit the institution, address the Grand Chancellor, Rue de Ville.

Paris is considered at present one of the best fortified cities in the world. In 1841 about forty million dollars were granted for completing the present fortifications. At about a mile and a half outside the former octroi walls runs a wall about forty-seven feet high, bastioned and terraced, in addition to which are seventeen outworks or forts, which include the principal suburbs of Paris, and command the approach in every direction. They are calculated for twenty-seven hundred and sixty gun-carriages, five hundred and seventy-four rampart guns, twenty-two hundred and thirty-eight mortars or cannons, and twenty thousand muskets. The fortifications have been greatly damaged during the two late sieges, and required a large amount of reparation.

Paris has a great many objects of interest to attract the attention of travelers. I consider it one of the most beautiful places in the world. Stayed at Paris four days.

GENEVA.

Geneva is beautifully situated at the southern extremity of Lake Geneva, on the banks of the Rhone. Contains forty-two thousand inhabitants. The Paix, kept by Mr. Koeler, long known as one of the best managers in Switzerland, is elegantly furnished, and commands a fine position. The people of Geneva are celebrated for their industry. Nearly four thousand persons are employed in the manufacture of watches, over seventy-five thousand being made yearly. Watches are much cheaper here than in America. The opportunity of purchasing these articles should not be lost. The house of Charles Martin & Co., Grand Quai, is justly celebrated for the excellence and accuracy of its time-keepers, its variety of chains, jewels, and music-boxes. They are guaranteed all gold of eighteen carats.

We went through the watch-factories, and saw

them make every wheel in the watch. Each person does one kind.

GENEVA LAKE.

We left Geneva by way of Geneva Lake, and then went to the head of the lake and through two other lakes, and then to Basle, which is situated on the banks of the Rhine. It is the capital of the canton, and contains forty-five thousand inhabitants.

STRASBOURG.

Went to Strasbourg, the chief city in the department Bas-Rhin. It contains seventy thousand inhabitants. The principal object of interest, and one to which most travelers resort after their arrival, is the Cathedral or Minster. This masterpiece of architecture is the work of Erwin von Steinbach, continued after his death by his son and daughter Sabina. It was begun in 1277 and finished in 1601. John Hultz, of Cologne, completed the work. The spire is remarkable as being the highest in the world, standing five hundred feet above the level of the Cathedral floor. It is twenty-five feet higher than the pyramid of Cheops, at Cairo, although the pyramid must have been about the same height, but has been worn away by the action of the atmosphere, the surface of the top being now about fifteen feet in diameter. The view from the top of the spire is most grand,—the winding of the Rhine, the Vosges Mountains of France, and the Black Forest of Germany, the scene of so many historical romances; a bird's-eye view of the whole panorama will reward the adventurous sight-seers. The ascent cannot be made without some danger, and requires considerable nerve and steadiness of head. The stone-work is so very open that in case of sudden attack of giddiness or slipping of the foot the body might pass through. There have been several such accidents. Two-thirds of the way up there is a watchman's station, where persons live, to keep a lookout for fires. Here a visitors' register is kept, and you can purchase prints, plans, and books descriptive of the Cathedral. The interior is rich in stained glass, but the most remarkable object of interest it contains is its world-renowned clock, invented three hundred years ago. It would fill a volume to describe it. When you visit it be particular to be present at twelve o'clock precisely, as that is the only time during the twelve hours when the cock crows and all the images, puppets, etc., are set in motion. I went to the top of the steeple twice, in 1851 and 1873. The Prussians during the late war fired balls into the Cathedral and damaged it very much. Stayed one day in Strasbourg.

BADEN BADEN.

Then to Baden Baden, the most beautiful watering-place in Germany; it is situated in a lovely valley, inclosed by the towering heights of the

Black Forest. The resident population is about six thousand; but, as many have it, forty thousand strangers have visited it in a single season. Gambling is all done away with; the government stopped it in 1851. I have seen men and women gamble from ten A.M. to eleven P.M. in the greatest style. Baden-Baden is the annual resort of idle pleasure-seekers and invalids from all parts of the world; its springs have been long and favorably known, even since the days of the Romans, and the new palace now belonging to the Grand Duke occupies the site of a Roman villa and bath. The water of the springs is warm; the principal one has a temperature of one hundred and fifty-three degrees Fahrenheit; the taste is saltish, and when drank as it issues from the spring, it resembles weak broth; it is very clear, but has a peculiar, disagreeable smell; the quality is saline, with a mixture of muriatic and carbonic acids, and small portions of silax and oxide of iron. The hot springs are thirteen in number. The portion of the town where they issue is called Hill; a building is erected over the principal spring. The vapor baths are situated back of the Catholic Church. Baths may be taken in all the various styles, including Russian baths. Here I took a Russian bath, which was most magnificent; there are six apartments. There are some eight or ten other baths, each having from ten to forty separate chambers. We stayed here two days, then went down the Rhine, and passed all the cities as far as Cologne.

COLOGNE.

Cologne is situated on the left side of the river, and contains one hundred and twenty-five thousand one hundred and seventy-two inhabitants. It is the capital of the province, and is the third city of importance in the Prussian Kingdom; it is built in the form of a crescent, close to the water, and is strongly fortified, the walls forming a circuit of nearly seven miles. Cologne is a place of great antiquity, and was of considerable importance during the Roman period. A Roman colony was planted in it by Agrippina, daughter of the Emperor Claudius, who was born here, and from its privileges as a Roman colony, Colonia Agrippina, the modern name of the city is preserved. During the Middle Ages, and for a long period of time, it was one of the most popular and important cities of Europe; it was also one of the chief cities of the Hanseatic League. The chief glory of Cologne is its magnificent Cathedral, or Minster, of St. Peter's, which is one of the most magnificent specimens of Gothic architecture in the world; although commenced in 1248, it is still unfinished. Its length is five hundred feet, which is to be the height of its two towers when finished; its width is two hundred and thirty feet; height of choir, one hundred and sixty-one feet. The work is now progressing rapidly; nearly two millions have been expended on it by the kings of Prussia during the last forty years. There is also a society established, with branches all over Europe, for the purpose of soliciting subscriptions for its completion; it is estimated that it will require about five million dollars for that purpose. Behind the high altar is the Chapel of the Magi, or the three Kings of Cologne. The custodian will tell you the silver case contains the bones of the three wise men who came from the East to Bethlehem to present their presents to the infant Christ, and that the case, which is ornamented with precious stones, and all the surrounding valuables in the chapel, are worth six million dollars. These remains were presented to the Archbishop of Cologne by the Emperor Barbarossa, who captured them at the city of Milan, which, at that time, possessed these valuable relics. The skulls of the Magi, crowned with diamonds, with their names written in rubies, are shown to the curious on payment of one dollar and thirty-seven cents for a party, on Sundays.

DUSSELDORF.

Went to Dusseldorf, on the right bank of the Rhine; it has now a population of over sixty-three thousand five hundred, which is fast increasing, many new and handsome residences being in course of erection, squares being laid out, and great improvements taking place daily. Dusseldorf, until the peace of Luneville, was a fortified town, some remains of which are still to be seen; but at the present time it is surrounded by gardens and pleasant walks. There is, however, a most remarkable collection of drawings by the old masters, of nearly fifteen thousand in number, including Raphael, Montagna, Guido, Romano, Domenichino, Michael Angelo, Titian, etc., also about three hundred and eighty water-color copies of the most remarbable paintings of the Italian school, from the fourth century, by Rautoul. Below this gallery is the public library, etc. From Cologne to Dusseldorf we passed many towns.

HANOVER.

Went to Hanover, situated in the midst of a sandy plain, upon the banks of the Leine, an affluent of the Weser; population, seventy-four thousand. There is nothing to be seen in Hanover of much importance, although it is the residence of the king. The streets of the new town are more regular, and lined with handsome houses.

BERLIN.

Went to Berlin, the capital of Prussia; contains seven hundred and five thousand inhabitants.

Berlin is situated on the river Spree, a small, sluggish stream, and is, ordinarily, the residence of the monarch; it is one of the largest and handsomest cities in Europe, being about twelve miles in circumference; it has a garrison of twenty thousand soldiers; the Spree intersects the city, insulating one of its quarters, and is crossed by more than fifty bridges in various parts of the city. The Spree is navigable for barges, and is connected, by means of canals, with the Oder as well as the Elbe, so that its internal water communication is extensive. Berlin is the first city of Germany for the variety of its manufacturing works; the principal are those of cloths, linen, carpets, silks, ribbons, and printed cottons, Berlin jewelry, paper, porcelain, and musical instruments. It is the greatest centre of instruction and intellectual development in Northern Germany; its libraries are large, and educational establishments very numerous. Its University, founded in 1809, comprising schools of Jurisprudence, Medicine, and Philosophy, has nearly two thousand scholars; it has an Academy of Fine Arts, an Academy of Sciences, an Academy for the Encouragement of Industry, an Academy of Music, a Geographical Society, a Society of Natural History, a Theological Seminary, schools of Artillery, Military Engineering, Architecture, Sculpture, Painting, and Music.

LEIPSIC.

Leipsic has ninety-one thousand inhabitants; it is the second city in Saxony, and one of the most industrious and commercial cities in Europe; it stands on a fertile plain near the right bank of the river Elster. Leipsic is a place of great historical celebrity and commercial importance, the money transactions often amounting to eighty millions of dollars. Leipsic is the centre of the German book trade, who, to the number of between six and seven hundred, meet here annually to balance their accounts, and their sales often amount to two millions of dollars yearly; nearly every bookseller or publisher in Germany has an agency here; there are about one hundred and thirty depots for books; fifteen steam-presses; the publishers have an exchange of their own, called the Buchhandler Börse, where they transact all their business.

DRESDEN.

Went to Dresden, the capital of the Kingdom of Saxony; it is delightfully situated on both banks of the Elbe; it has one hundred and fifty-six thousand inhabitants. The city has the great advantage of possessing an American club, at No. 22 Victoria Street, where the latest American papers can be found, and where a list is kept of all Americans visiting Dresden. Martin Luther was born 10th of November, 1483, in Eisleben, a town in Prussian Saxony; he was the son of a miner; he studied at Eisenach, begging, in the mean time, to obtain a subsistence. A thunderbolt having killed one of his companions at his side caused him to embrace religion; he entered the convent of the

Augustines and became professor of theology in the University of Wittenberg. Having studied the writings of John Huss, he rapidly acquired a taste for his opinions; the sale of indulgences by the Pope furnished him a reason to open the controversy. He published an argument, in which he denied their efficacy; the quarrel soon became violent. ·Luther, who at first attacked but the abuses of the church, now attacked the authority of the Pope, the belief in purgatory, the celibacy of the priests, the possession of temporal wealth, the doctrine of transubstantiation, and the mass. He married a nun, named Catharina von Bora, by whom he had six children. He was excommunicated by the Pope, and Henry VIII. of England wrote strongly against him. He burnt the bulls of the Pope, and responded to Henry VIII. in the strongest terms. The Duchy of Saxony, Denmark, and Sweden took the part of Luther in this quarrel. At the Diet of Worms, he supported his opinions.

PRAGUE.

We now resume our route from Dresden to Prague. This city, the capital of Bohemia, stands in a basin, surrounded on all sides by rocks and eminences, upon the slopes of which the buildings rise tier after tier as they recede from the water's brink. It contains one hundred and forty-five thousand inhabitants, and, next to Vienna, is the most important place in the German provinces of Austria, and ranks next to the capital in point of size and population. Prague stands on both sides of the Moldau (the chief tributary of the Elbe), in the centre of the province, and in the midst of a fertile and beautiful region. It is the chief seat of the manufacturing industry of Bohemia, and a place of great inland trade. This is facilitated by its extensive railway communication, which gives its citizens immediate intercourse with Vienna on one side and with all the great cities of northern and western Germany in another direction. There is a gorgeous silver shrine, weighing nearly four thousand pounds, placed in the Cathedral of St. Vitus. We now go to Vienna, the capital of the Austrian Empire. It is situated on a plain five hundred feet above the level of the sea, but very little above the level of the Danube, near whose southern bank it is situated. Population, nine hundred thousand.

VIENNA.

Vienna, for its wealth and size, comes nearer London and Paris than any other European city. It differs from these cities in this respect, that it preserves about it more antique grandeur, and that it is the old and not the new parts of the city that form the fashionable quarters and contain most of the objects of interest which Vienna presents to the stranger, including beside the Imperial Palace those of Prince Esterhazy, Lichtenstein, Metternich, Schwarzenberg, and Auersberg, as well as the principal churches, museum galleries, libraries, and public offices of every kind. There is no city in Europe has so large a number of resident nobility as Vienna. There are nearly two hundred families of princes, counts, and barons who make Vienna their residence the greater part of the year, spending from fifty thousand to two hundred thousand dollars yearly. It is said that with the exception of London, the citizens of Vienna are the richest in Europe. Vienna is also noted for its Bohemian glass manufacture. Here at Vienna was the World's Fair, which was the most splendid affair in the world. We stayed there eight days.

MUNICH.

We then went to Munich, the capital of Bavaria. It is situated on the left bank of the river Isar, nearly seventeen hundred feet above the level of the sea. It contains one hundred and seventy-seven thousand inhabitants. Munich is considered, in proportion to its size, one of the finest cities of Europe, and, with the exception perhaps of Florence and Madrid, shines conspicuously above all the others in regard to its extensive collection of works of art, principally brought together under the care of Ludwig, late king of Bavaria, to the Dusseldorf gallery, removed here by Max Joseph, and the Manheim collection, transferred to Munich by the Elector Palatine, added to the galleries of Nuremburg, Bamberg, Augsburg, Walenstine, and Broisseree. It is also rich in public buildings of various kinds, and has numerous gardens, squares, and monuments. In the Hall of Founders the walls are hung with the portraits of the sovereigns who have contributed most largely to the formation of the gallery, viz., the Electors Maximilian I., Max, Emanuel, Johann, Wilhelm, founder of the Dusseldorf gallery, Karl Theodore of the Palatinate, and the Kings Maximilian, Joseph, and Ludwig.

Made our way to Innspruck, which is the capital of the Tyrol, and contains fourteen thousand inhabitants. The Hôtel de Autriche is the best, and is admirably managed; for the last three years it has been conducted by M. F. Baer. The city is situated on the banks of the river Inn, and is nearly inclosed with mountains, varying from six to ten thousand feet in height. The river is crossed by two bridges, one of wood and the other a handsome suspension bridge of recent construction.

INNSPRUCK.

The principal object of attraction in Innspruck are the tomb of Maximilian I. in the Hofkirche, in the church of the Franciscans, one of the finest monuments in Europe; a sight of it alone will repay a visit to Tyrol. The monument is situated in the centre of the church, and consists of a high marble sarcophagus on which the effigy of Maximilian I., in bronze, appears kneeling. The statue is by Ludovic del Duea. On the sides of the sarcophagus are twenty-four relics in marble, representing the principal events in the life of the emperor; Nos. 8, 9, 10, and 11 are considered the finest specimens of Alexander Colin, of Mechlin, who executed from No. 1 to 20; from No. 21 to 24 were executed by Barnard Abel, of Cologne; No. 8, the return of Margaret, Maximilian's daughter, from France, is most exquisitely executed. Stayed there one day, and then made our way to Verona, Padua, and Venice through the Apennine Mountains; passed through forty-five tunnels before we got to Verona.

VENICE.

Venice, a famous maritime city of united Italy, formerly the capital of the republic of the same name; population, one hundred and twenty thousand. The city of Venice, formerly called the Queen of the Adriatic, is unrivaled as to beauty and situation; it stands on the bay, near the Gulf of Venice; in this gulf, or Adriatic Sea, the ceremony of espousing the Adriatic took place annually, on Ascension-day; it was performed by the doge, accompanied by all the nobility and ambassadors in gondolas, dropping into the sea a ring from his state barge. This ceremony was omitted, for the first time in many centuries, in 1797. Venice is situated upon seventy-two islands; its peculiar formation renders it singularly attractive; the islands, upon which the city is built, lie in the midst of extensive lagoons, which surround it on all sides. The access to the city is very difficult; a great portion of the lagoon, on which it is situated, being dry at low water, merchant vessels usually moor off the Ducal Palace; sometimes, however, they come into the Grand Canal, which intersects the city. In consequence of the chain of long, narrow islands, which bounds the lagoon on the side next to the sea, being in part broken away, the republic, during the last century, was obliged to construct a mole, seven miles in length, to protect the city and port from storms and the swell of the Adriatic. This vast work is admired for its extent and solidity; it is formed of blocks of Italian marble, and connects various little islands and towns; the principal from the sea to the lagoon is at Malamocco, one and one-half leagues from the city; there is a bar outside of Malamocco, on which there is not more than ten feet of water at the spring tides; on arriving at the bar, ships are conducted across it and into port by pilots, whose service must be availed of. The Grand Canal, which takes a serpentine course through the city, is intersected by one hundred and forty-six smaller canals, over which there are three hundred and six bridges, which, being very steep and intended only for foot passengers, are cut into steps on either side; these canals, crossed by bridges, form the water streets of Venice; the greater part of the intercourse of the city being carried on by means of gondolas, supplying the place of coaches or carriages. Even horse-back riding is wholly out of the question here, the streets are so very narrow, not usually over four to five feet in width, with the exception of the Merceria, which is from twelve to twenty feet across, in the centre of the city, and is lined on either side with handsome stores. The gondola is therefore the mode of conveyance; it cuts its way so rapidly through the water that in a short time you may be able to visit every part of the city; these are long, narrow, light vessels, painted black, according to an ancient law, containing in the centre a cabin, nicely fitted up with glass windows, blinds, cushions, etc.; those belonging to private families are much more richly decorated. One gondolier is generally considered sufficient, and the price is then four lire per day, but double that fare for two rowers. The most pleasant and healthy portions of Venice are in the vicinity of the Grand Canal, which is broad and deep, on either side of which are magnificent palaces and churches; it varies from one hundred to one hundred and eighty feet in width, and is crossed by the principal bridges, among which is the famous

Rialto, which was built of marble by Antonio Da Ponte, in 1591, and, like other bridges of Venice, has stairs by which people ascend on one side and descend on the other; the view from this bridge is remarkably fine: the beauties of Grecian architecture meet the eye of the stranger on every side he feels disposed to turn. It is eighty-nine feet in span, and is divided into three parts,—a narrow street running through the centre, with shops on either side, and two still narrower between the shops and balustrade; its appearance is heavy, and by no means merits the great fame and attention which it has excited.

The manufactures of Venice are much more various than many persons suppose; the glassworks situated on the island of Murano employing about four hundred hands, who are engaged in arranging beads, produce magnificent mirrors, artificial pearls, colored beads, etc.; gold chains, and every variety of jewelry is also produced extensively, together with gold and silver materials, velvets, silks, laces, and other valuable goods. Venice was the earliest, and, for a long time, the most extensive commercial city in Europe; her origin dates from the invasion of Italy by Attila, in 452. In the fifteenth century, Venice was considered by far the richest and most magnificent city of Europe, with the single exception of Rome, and those who visited her were impressed with still higher notions of her grandeur on account of her singular situation in the midst of the sea. There are magnificent views in Venice of all descriptions. Stayed in Venice three days.

ROME.

After passing forty-five tunnels through the Apennine Mountains, we started for Rome, the most celebrated of European cities, famous in both ancient and modern history; formerly, for being the most powerful nation of antiquity; afterward, the ecclesiastical capital of Christendom and the residence of the Pope, and since 1871 the capital of united Italy and the residence of the king. It is situated on both banks of the Tiber, about sixteen miles from its mouth; population, two hundred and fifty thousand, having decreased about one hundred thousand in twenty-two years. It is impossible, in a visit as brief as that usually given to the ancient capital of the civilized world, to become thoroughly acquainted with its objects of interest. Within its walls, and in the range of a few miles around it, is found the greater part of the material on which we base our knowledge of the antique; within a day's ride are the remains of all the epochs of civilization of which we have any knowledge, and in the galleries, composed of the remains found in and around Rome, is the most of what we have of antique art. The first object of interest as we approach the city in an irregular, zigzag structure, mainly of brick, with towers and bastions of all forms and kinds of masonry; it is that known as the wall of Aurelius; it has been breached and repaired many times, and was thoroughly repaired by Belisarius, since whose time it has undergone little change. It probably coincided with the more ancient wall of Servius Tullius only at one point, near St. John Lateran. Incorporated within the course of its circuit are the pyramid of Caius Cestius, the soldiers' amphitheatre, the aqueducts, and the Prætorian camp. It had, on the Capitol side of the Tiber, thirteen gates, of which eight only remain, and on the Vatican side two, of which only one, with a portion of the wall, remains. The actual wall of the Vatican part of the city is of Middle Age construction. The Porta St. Lorenzo is by far the earlier and much the more interesting. The inscription on the Porta Maggiore, together with the several aqueducts passing over it, have great interest; the architecture of the gate being, however, very bad. The railway enters the city by an opening made for its passage near the Porta Maggiore, and has its terminus at the Piazza Di Termini, the site of the baths of Diocletian, of which some magnificent fragments will give the traveler his first evidences of the splendor of Rome of the emperors. The railway passes between two most interesting ruins between the wall and the terminus,—the temple of Minerva Medica and the

Agger of Servius Tullius, supposed formerly to have been here only a mound, but shown by the cutting of the railway through it to contain a massive Etruscan wall of huge blocks of peperino. The wall of Servius Tullius inclosed the seven hills, and, passing from the Quirinal to the Capitol, struck the Tiber near the island; the greater part of modern Rome having been built on what was anciently the Campus Martius and adjacent land lying outside the Servian wall; in fact, the seven hills are almost entirely uninhabited. The Arentine, overlooking the Tiber and port of Rapa Grande, having on it only two monastic establishments, the Palatine, the ruins of the palace of the Cæsars (now being partially excavated), and two monastic buildings, the Cælian, the Villa Mattei, now a nunnery, the churches of St. Stefano Rotonda, St. Gregory, St. John, and Paul, the ruins of Vivarium, and a few buildings, monastic and other, on the side toward the Esquiline; on the latter are the ruins of the Baths of Titus, St. Pertio in Vincoli, and two or three farm-houses; the Quirinal is traversed by the Via di Quattrofontane, but the greater part of it is occupied by the grounds of the Villa Negroni, the Baths of Diocletian, and vineyards, parts of the Quirinal and Capitol only being to any extent dwelt on. Of the bridges which cross the Tiber, the Ponte St. Angelo, formerly Pons Ælins, built by Adrian; Cisto, formerly Jamcolensis, Quattro Capi, formerly Fabricius, connecting the island with the city; St. Bartolomeo, formerly Cestius, and Ponte Rotto, formerly Palatinus, of which a part only remains, the damage being repaired by a suspension bridge, the work of Pius IX., are all ancient.

A suspension bridge near the Santo Spirito is the only entirely modern one, while of the Subliems, made immortal by Horatius Cœles, and the first built across the Tiber, and of the Triumphalis, which led to the Temple of Jupiter Vaticanus, only the remains of the piers are left; the latter visible from the point St. Angelo, the former from Marmorata, a marble depot beneath the Arentine. The first visit of most travelers will be to the Forum Romanum and the adjacent ruins, and certainly in a few acres which lie between the Capitol and the Colosseum is gathered the most marvelous collection of the remains of antiquity to be found in the world.

From the Cloaca Maxima, and Mamertine prison, the work of the early kings, built nearly twenty-five centuries ago, down to the Balsilica of Constantine, we have an almost complete series of the building of all epochs; the Forum itself, in the valley between the Palatine and Capitoline hills, being the nucleus, as if Rome grouped all her most glorious works around the cradle of her power, the place of her popular assemblies.

The Amphitheatre, known as the Colosseum, is said to have given seats to eighty-seven thousand spectators, and was inaugurated A.D. 81, the same year in which Titus died; on which occasion five thousand wild animals and ten thousand captives were slain; the inauguration lasted one hundred days. There are three orders of architecture used in the four stories,—the first, Doric; the second, Ionic; the third and fourth, Corinthian; in each of the lower tiers there were eighty arches. The circumference of the building is one thousand six hundred and forty-one feet; the height of the outer wall, one hundred and fifty-seven feet; the length of the arena is two hundred and seventy-eight feet, and width, one hundred and seventy-seven feet; the whole superficial area is six acres. The Capitol, the Pantheon, the temple of Neptune, the church of St. Nicola in Carcere, the many theatres and amphitheatres formerly existing in Rome, the remains of the public baths, are the most impressive ruins of Rome, excepting the Colosseum, the ancient tombs, and St. Peter's Church, which is one of the greatest buildings in the world; we were on the top of the steeple. We stayed at Rome five days, and then proceeded to Naples.

NAPLES.

Naples has a population of six hundred thousand souls; it has three hundred thousand inhabitants more than it had in 1851 (it is now 1873). It is a fine city. The next morning after arriving we went to Vesuvius and Pompeii, and found them very interesting. The early history of Pompeii is involved in obscurity, but the supposition is that it was settled by Osci and Pelasgi, prior to the establishment on this coast of the Greek colonies, about the year 440 B.C., and was taken by the Romans eighty years afterwards. During the Social war it revolted with the other Campanian towns, and but little more was known respecting it until it was visited by an earthquake A.D. 63, which occasioned great destruction; it was afterward overwhelmed in 79 by an eruption of Vesuvius, and continued to be buried under the ashes and other volcanic matter for about sixteen hundred and sixty-nine years, notwithstanding that the celebrated architect and engineer, Domenico Fatlana, who was employed in constructing an aqueduct to convey water to Torre, fell in with the ruins of the city. No particular attention was paid to the discovery until 1748, since which time it has continued to be an object of great interest, and since 1755 the progress of excavation has been pretty constantly prosecuted. The walls of the city are twenty feet thick and about twenty feet high, faced with blocks of lava inside and out; there are six gates, and many towers rising above the ramparts and pierced with arches; but the best means of approach to Pompeii is afforded by the Appian Way to the gate of Herculaneum. Along either side of the road, approaching this gate, are a number of ancient tombs, many of which are in as perfect a state as though they had been erected at a more recent period; they recall the ancient glories of the Appian, and the road is called the Street of the Tombs, through which we will pass and note the most important objects. Many of the houses have derived their names from the paintings which they contained, and in many cases from the royal personages in whose honor the excavations have been made. The Herculaneum Gate, the most important entrance to the city, had a central archway, twenty feet in height and fifteen in width; it was of purely Roman architecture, built alternately of bricks and lava. On the outside of this gate is a fine specimen of ancient masonry,—one of the best preserved portions of the walls of Pompeii. The Temple of Venus, the most superb of all the temples in Pompeii, is situated on the west side of the Forum, and occupies an area of one hundred and fifty feet by seventy-five.

The great or tragic Theatre, supposed to have been capable of containing five thousand persons, was erected in an elevated position, and escaped, in a great measure, the devastation which swept over other houses situated on the plain. We stayed at Naples four days, and then took a steamer, line Di Egetts, from Naples to Alexandria, Egypt, via Messino; from there to Cairo, to see the pyramids of Gheezeh.

ALEXANDRIA.

September 1, 1873.—My traveling companion, Rev. A. F. Shanafelt, and myself embarked at Naples, on board the steamship Egypt, of the Buliauna line, for Alexandria, Egypt; found the vessel inferior in all her appointments. Our course over the Mediterranean took us within near view of the celebrated volcanic mountain Stromboli. In due time we entered the Strait of Messina, with Mount Etna in the distance. After five and a half days of rough sailing we reached Alexandria, and here our hearts were saddened with the intelligence that we were to be quarantined on account of the cholera in Geneva; we were treated more like dogs than men; our bread sour and not served with any regularity. Not being able to speak any language but English added greatly to our discomfort. Our fellow-passengers were French, Italians, Turks, and Arabians; only one English-speaking individual beside ourselves. We longed for liberty; it might come in a day, and maybe not for weeks; painfully were we reminded that we were under Alexandrian and not American rule. When released from the prison, we hoped to continue our journey through Palestine and Syria, with a view to returning home in November next. Around the prison were hundreds of trees laden with ripe figs, but we could not reach them. Our beds were upon the stone; nothing but a cot, and no chair or stool to rest ourselves upon; the floors are all laid with stone, and I suppose the prison would accommodate five hundred persons; in its form it is circular.

Alexandria is the seaport and commercial capital of Egypt, and contains about three hundred thousand inhabitants. The buildings that come one by one into view constitute Alexandria, and the tall column that first attracts the stranger's view is Pompey's Pillar. This city was founded by Alexander the Great 332 years before Christ; it is admirably situated between the west mouth of the Nile and Lake Mareolis; is connected with the Rosetta mouth of the Nile by the Mahmoodeeyeh Canal, reopened in 1819 by Mohammed Ali; the length of the canal is forty-eight miles. The modern city is partly built on the celebrated island of Pharos, and the isthmus connects it with the main-land; the ancient city was built on the main-land opposite the present site. Alexandria has two ports,—that on the west, which is the best, is called the Old Harbor, and that on the east the New. The population is mixed; beside the native Turks and Arabs we have Americans, Greeks, Syrians, Jews, Maltese, and Europeans of almost every nation in such numbers that it may be questioned whether the strangers you notice in the streets would not be more than a match for the natives; the shops display every article of furniture, and of male and female attire, from the Parisian bonnet to the very humblest article of dress; all conspire in conjunction with the style of the buildings to take away from this place the appearance of an oriental city. The name given Pompey's Pillar is without historical foundation, as the Greek inscription found upon it proves it to have been erected by Publius, Prefect of Egypt, in honor of Diocletian, who besieged Alexandria A.D. 296; that the city, after a defense lasting eight months, was obliged to capitulate, and thousands perished by fire and sword. The height of the Pillar, including the shaft, capital, and pedestal, is one hundred feet; it is of red polished granite, elegant and in good style, but the capital and pedestal are inferior and unfinished. Cleopatra's Needles, those two obelisks which may be seen near the eastern part of the city, near the shore, the one standing, the other lying down and nearly covered with earth, are of red granite, and formerly stood before the Temple of Neptune, at Heliopolis. One of them is sixty-five feet, and the other seventy; their diameter at base is eight feet; they were quarried in the reign of Thothmes III., 1495 B.C., and are consequently now three thousand three hundred and sixty-three years old; Mohammed Ali gave the fallen one to the British Government, but they concluded it was hardly worth the money it would cost to remove it. At the catacombs, a distance of about three miles from the hotel, may be seen those remarkable tombs; they may be reached by either land or sea; if by land, which is preferable, we pass some ancient tombs, partly sunk in the sea.

CAIRO.

We left Alexandria the 12th day of September, 1873, for Cairo, one hundred and thirty-five miles, passing a great many towns of inferior grade. The population of Cairo, at the time of the French expedition, in 1779, was estimated at two hundred thousand; since then it has been gradually increasing, and, according to the last returns, it now amounts, including the suburbs and Boolac and Old Cairo, to about three hundred and eighty thousand inhabitants. The manufacture and industry of Cairo consists in gold and silver jewelry, silk and cotton stuffs, embroidery, native saddles, etc.; many European industries have lately been introduced; a return, published in 1871, gives the number of people employed in different occupations; the most numerous corporation are the porters, 14,500; then come the vendors of eatables, 12,000; glaziers, 10,000; donkey- and camel-drivers, 8000, and so on, including, among others, 4000 water-carriers, 3500 coffee-house keepers, 3200 barbers, 3000 goldsmiths, 1200 chicken-rearers, 1100 hotel-keepers, 300 coffee and tobacco cutters, down to 35 plumbers; this list is probably more curious than accurate, but it will serve to give some idea of the principal occupations followed. The hatching of eggs by artificial heat has been carried on in Egypt since the time of the Pharaohs; one of the principal egg-hatching ovens, called, in Arabic, Maamatel Fatakh, is at Cairo; the peasants supply the eggs, and generally receive one chicken for every two eggs; chicken-eggs require twenty days, turkey, 30 days. The citadel (El Kalah) was built by Saladin, in 1166, of stone brought from small pyramids at Gheezeh, and formed part of his general plan for strengthening the town and protecting it from assault; but it can hardly be said to have been well chosen for this object, as it is completely commanded by Mount Mokkatam, and it was by erecting a battery in the fort on the projecting point, called Gabel ej Josshee, immediately behind it, that Mohammed Ali compelled the surrender of the citadel, then in possession of Khoorshia Pasha. According to the Arab historians of the day, however, Saladin is said to have fixed on the spot because it was found that meat kept fresh there twice as long as anywhere else in Cairo. The city side is well defended by the natural abruptness of the rocks, and is also strongly armed and regularly fortified. A good carriage-road leads up from the open square, called Er Rumeyleh, to the principal outer entrance gate, and continues on through another gate into the interior of the citadel; another way is by the Babel Azab, a fine massive gateway, flanked by two enormous towers; it was in this narrow and tortuous lane, leading from this gate, that the massacre of the Mamelukes took place, by order of Mohammed Ali, on the 1st of March, 1811. As soon as they had passed through the Babel Azab, it and the upper gate were shut, and they were thus caught in a trap; all were shot, except one Emir boy, who escaped by leaping his horse over a breach in their dilapidated wall; the spot is, however, a little to the north of the Babel Azab; there was probably a large accumulation of rubbish below the gap, which broke the fall, which was twenty-five feet. The citadel is in itself a small town, and contains many objects worth seeing. The palace, built by Mohammed Ali, which has taken the place of the old palace of Saladin, contains some very handsome rooms, especially a bath-room all of alabaster; the view from some of the rooms is very fine; the building is now, with the exception of a part occupied by the prince hereditary, only used for state receptions; the ministerial divans, which used to have their offices in it, have now been moved to the west end of the city. The old palace of Saladin, commonly called Joseph's Hill, was pulled down in 1829 to make room for the new Mosque of Mohammed Ali; here we could see Joseph's Well, where he used to drink of the water; the well is about two hundred and sixty feet deep. The most remarkable object in this place is the vast hall, supported on thirty-two columns of rose granite taken from the ancient temples, but the columns were broken when the building was pulled down; the two minarets, still standing to the east of the mosque, formed a part of the Mosque of Kalaron, which stood in the centre of the palace court. The Mosque of Mohammed Ali was commenced by that prince, but not finished till after his death; it consists of an open square, surrounded by a single row of columns, ten on the north and south, thirteen on the west, and twelve on the east, where a door leads to the inner part, or house of prayer, as in the Tooloon and other mosques of similar plan. The columns have a fancy capital, supporting round arches, and the whole, with the exception of the outer walls, is oriental alabaster; but it has not the pure oriental character of other works in Cairo, and it excites the admiration for the materials rather than for the style of its architecture; its minarets, too, which are of the Turkish order, are painfully elongated, in defiance of all proportion; they interfere with the very appearance of all around them, and that, too, in the city remarkable for so many elegant models of Saracenic time. The decorations of the interior are in very bad taste, and the large

European lustre, hanging from the roof, with the wretched lanterns strung about in every direction, helps to offend the eye; the vast size and the richness of the material produce, however, on the whole, a fine effect, and it is well worth seeing when lighted up in the evening. Immediately on the right, on entering, is the tomb of the founder. On entering this magnificent temple, we had to take boots off and put on slippers, before we went into the church, and so it is with every one that enters. On the east side of the citadel hill is Joseph's Well; it is probable that the original well was hewn in the rock by the ancient Egyptians, like the tanks on the hill behind the citadel, near the Kobbet el Hawa, and this is rendered more probable from there having been, as has been said, an old town, called Louirkeshiomi, on the site of the modern city. The well consists of two parts, the upper of which is about one hundred and sixty feet deep, and the lower one hundred and sixty, making a total of three hundred and twenty feet; the bottom of the well is supposed to correspond with the level of the Nile; the water is raised by bullocks, or donkeys, to the top; the water is also brought to the citadel by the aqueduct direct from the Nile at Old Cairo. We visited the museum of Antiquities, the objects of which may be classed under five heads: religious monuments, funeral monuments, civil monuments, historical monuments, Greek and Roman monuments; it is one of the finest perhaps in the world. An excursion to the petrified forest, made from Cairo, will take from four to five hours; the tombs of the Caliphs (Kaid Bey) may be taken in the way, or it may be combined with the excursion to Heliopolis. It is a somewhat wearisome ride, and a still more wearisome drive, when, as is often the case, the carriage sticks in the sand, and neither blows, prayers, or curses are effectual in getting the wretched horses to move. A donkey-ride is the best way of getting there, and to those who do not care to take the trouble to ride, it may be said, it is not worth while to drive there. After passing Kaid Bey, the way lies along a sandy road, with the Gabel el Ahmar on the left, and the Jebel Mokkatam on the right; the Gabel el Ahmar, or red mountain, is composed of red gritstone, which runs into a silicious rock, and is of the same nature as the Vocal Statue at Thebes. Owing to the quality of the stone, which renders it peculiarly adapted for mills, this mountain has been quarried from a very early period to the present day, as may be seen from the fragments at Heliopolis. The same species of rock rises here and there to the southward upon the slope of the limestone range, and the bed above it contains petrified wood in abundance. Here are open volcanoes from eight to fifty feet, where the lava was thrown up to a great amount, and the petrified wood is as hard as stone; it is about eight miles to the bed of petrified wood from Cairo. From here we went to Heliopolis Pyramids, and saw where Joseph and Mary sat under the sycamore-tree, or Joseph's tree, resting themselves; near there we saw a pyramid supposed to be from four to five thousand years old. Most of the people in Egypt are Arabs, mulatto, and some dark; the women have their faces covered. Old Cairo is about three miles from Cairo; it is the Roman fortress of Babylon.

BABYLON.

Here Babylon was anciently built, according to tradition, and we can see many of the old walls. Here we go out to the pyramidical platform of Gheezeh, the great pyramid, the second pyramid, the third pyramid, and the other small pyramids, the Sphinx, causeways, tombs, pyramid of Aboorsash, pyramid of Abooser, and many other places of interest.

PYRAMIDS.

The dimensions of the great pyramid have been stated at different times by ancient and modern writers. Herodotus makes it eight hundred feet in length on each side at the base, and the same in height. Pliny gives the length as eight hundred and eighty-three feet, and the same in height. The space covered by this pyramid is said to equal the area of Lincoln's Inn Fields, England, and its solid contents have been calculated at eighty-five million cubic feet. Having reached the pyramid, the next thing is to accomplish the task which most travelers think it necessary to set for themselves,—getting to the top of it. The ascent is usually made from the northeast corner, near the chalet which was built by the Khedive for the visit of the Prince and Princess of Wales, in 1868. Some pronounce getting to the top fatiguing, while others declare it is the easiest thing possible. Three strong and respectable-looking Arabs took me in charge, and we soon arrived at the top of the pyramid, seven hundred feet; we found a coffin where one of the princes had been buried in a large room, say twenty feet square. Along the side of the wall there are holes to let in the air. We left Cairo on the morning of the 12th of September; passed through the Desert of Egypt. Not a tree, shrub, or spear of grass was to be seen anywhere. Nothing but sand and gravel; mountains of sand one hundred feet high.

SUEZ.

To Suez, one hundred and ninety miles from Cairo, on the Red Sea. This is a small town. Here we took passage on a boat for five miles; then rode a donkey seven miles, to Moses's Well or Springs; there are seven of them; then we went to where the children of Israel crossed the Red Sea, which, I suppose, is five miles wide; perhaps one million people passed through the Red Sea when the waters were parted, and the Egyptians passed after them, and were drowned. Stayed at Suez two nights, and then went back the same road eighty miles to Ismalia.

PORT SAID.

There took a steamboat and went to Port Said, a small town on the Mediterranean Sea; through the Suez Canal; through the Desert of Egypt on one side and the Desert of Arabia on the other side; distance eighty miles; no kind of vegetation on the soil. This canal is one of the greatest improvements I ever saw anywhere. It connects the Red Sea and the Mediterranean together. Heretofore travelers had to go a long distance to reach Port Said, but now we took passage at Ismalia at four o'clock P.M., and reached Port Said about ten o'clock in the morning. Here we were disappointed by a steamer not leaving Port Said until two days for Jaffa. Hotels are not good in any of these cities. From here we started for Jaffa, on the Mediterranean Sea, about four o'clock P.M. We had a pleasant passage to Jaffa, where we arrived safely.

JOPPA OR JAFFA.

Jerusalem, September 22, 1873.—I give you an account of Joppa or Jaffee, now called Yaffa by the Franks of Jaffa.

Joppa is a beautiful town on an inclining hill dipping into the Mediterranean, and encompassed on the land side by orchards of oranges, lemons, citrons, and apricots, scarcely surpassed in the world. Like most oriental towns, however, Joppa looks better at a distance. The houses are huddled together without regard to appearance or convenience. The streets form a labyrinth of blind alleys and narrow, crooked, filthy lanes, and the whole town is so crowded along the steep sides of the hill that the rickety mansions on the upper part seem to be toppling over on the flat roofs of those below them. Still it has an air of bustle and thrift about it which makes some amends for the want of architectural finish and its dirt. It has no port, and it is only under favorable circumstances a vessel can lie a mile or two from the shore. Many a time the steamers pass without being able to land either mail or passengers. There is indeed a place along the shore which has sometimes been dignified by the name of harbor. It consists of a strip of water from forty to fifty feet wide and from five to ten feet deep, surrounded on the sea side by low and partially sunken rocks. It has two entrances on the west ten feet wide, and the other on the north not much larger. Such a spot may afford a little shelter to open boats, but is worse than useless so far as commerce is concerned. The town is dignified by a wall, on which a few old guns are mounted toward the sea. On the land side there is but one gate, and it is always so crowded with donkeys, camels, and lazy Arabs, that one has difficulty in forcing his way through. Just within it is a fountain, adorned with a profusion of carving and Arabic inscriptions. The bazaars are well supplied with excellent fruit, especially oranges, for which Joppa is the most celebrated in Syria. It contains about five thousand inhabitants, of whom one thousand are Christians, about one hundred and fifty Jews, and the rest Moslems. French steamers call every ten days, bringing European mails from Alexandria, and proceeding northward to Beyrout and Constantinople; also at similar intervals taking mails to Alexandria for Europe. Austrian steamers likewise call once a week. Travelers arriving at Joppa, to travel inland, will find horses and mules to carry them and their baggage to Jerusalem, where further arrangements can easily be made. Those not as yet provided with a dragoman will find Jew boys about the harbor with enough of some known tongue to interpret your wants. With the exception of a few granite columns and some old stones built up in the walls, chiefly raised from the palace of Ascalon, there are no remains of antiquity in Joppa. There are three mosques and three small convents, Latin, Greek, and Armenian. Joppa is traditionally the oldest city in the world, for Pliny says it existed before the flood, and even historically it is a place of high antiquity. Among the towns allotted to the tribe of Dan we find the name of Joppa,—a remarkable instance of the tenacity of Shemitic names. It next appears as the port at which the floats of cedar and pine from Lebanon for the building of the temple were landed. I suppose you remember Joppa. I do very well. When the Joppa is mentioned after the return from captivity, Ezra tells us the Jews gave meat and drink and oil unto them of Zidon and to them of Tyre to bring cedar-trees from Lebanon to the sea of Joppa, for rebuilding the house of the Lord; and it was at Joppa Jonah embarked for Tarshish; here, too, Peter raised Tabitha from the dead, and resided many days in the house of Simon the tanner—the house is shown; and it was here that while praying on the housetop he saw the strange vision of clean and unclean beasts and creeping things, and heard a voice saying, " Rise, Peter, kill and eat." Joppa is frequently mentioned in the wars of Maccabees, and on one occasion, when its inhabitants had thrown two hundred Jews into the sea, Judas, in revenge, surprised and burned the Syrian fleet that lay before it. During the Roman wars, Joppa was burned by Constantine, and upwards of eight thousand of its inhabitants were butchered. It was made the seat of a bishop in the time of Constantine, and retained the honor till its conquest by the Saracens, in 636. It was an important port during the Crusades, but from that time till the close of the past century its history is obscure and uninteresting. Then, however, its name rang throughout Europe and Asia as the scene of one of the bloodiest tragedies on record. On the 4th of March, 1799, Joppa was invested by the French, under Napoleon. In two days a breach was made by the cannon, and the town was carried by storm and delivered over to all the horrors of war, which never appeared in a form more frightful. During this scene of slaughter a large part of the garrison, consisting chiefly of Albanians, took refuge in some old khans, and called out from the windows that they would lay down their arms, provided their lives were spared, but otherwise they would fight till the last extremity. Two officers, Eugene Beauharnais and Crosier, Napoleon's own aids-de-camp, agreed to the proposal, and brought them out disarmed in two bodies; one consisting of twenty-five hundred men and the other fifteen hundred. On reaching headquarters, Napoleon received them with stern demeanor, and expressed his highest indignation against his aids-de-camp for attempting to burden him with such a body of prisoners. They were made to sit down in front of the tents with their hands tied behind their backs. Despair was already pictured in every face, for the relentless frown of the general and the gloomy whispers of the officers could not be mistaken; but no cry was uttered, no semblance of cowardice exhibited. With calm resignation characteristic of the Moslem spirit and faith, they yielded to their fate. Bread and water were served out to them, while a council of war was summoned to deliberate. For two days the terrible question of life or death was debated. Justice and common humanity were not without their advocates, but savage barbarity, under the name of political necessity, prevailed. The committee to whom the matter was referred unanimously reported that they should be put to death, and Napoleon immediately signed the fatal order. They were massacred to a man, on the 10th of March, 1799. Here we had to take a dragoman, a native of Alexandria. At Joppa we took four horses, eight mules, two donkeys, four common servants, one waiter, Abraham, one cook, Emanuel, one dragoman, Stustapha H. Mussa. He had a wife, named Hei, in London, while at school. He is a full-blooded Arab, yellow, but his wife is a smart, intelligent woman. They have one child, and it is Arab.

We took a ride in Alexandria in a carriage for six miles together. We had two guards from Jerusalem, with muskets, swords, pistols, and clubs. There was one man murdered near the sea a few days ago. Every party that is traveling carries muskets, pistols, swords, and clubs, for protection.

RAMLEH.

We now leave Joppa for Ramleh; the houses of this place are well built, not so closely packed as in most oriental towns, but running out into the orchards; the streets are tolerably clean; the population is estimated at three thousand; two-thirds Moslems, and the rest Christians. The town is comparatively modern, possessing few buildings or ruins earlier than the time of the Crusades; but the chief architectural attraction of Ramleh is a beautiful tower, which stands on high ground, one-fourth of a mile out of the town; around it are the remains of a large, quadrangular inclosure, once a spacious khan, like those found along the leading roads in the country; some of the arches of the curiosities are still standing, and in the centre of the area are extensive vaults; the tower is now isolated, but there can be little doubt that it was at one time attached to a mosque. Most of the great khans in Syria had their mosques and minarets, and a few of them may still be seen near other places. The tower is Saracenic, square, and beautifully built; the angles are supported by slender buttresses, and the sides taper upwards in stories. A narrow, winding staircase, lighted by pointed windows, leads to the top, where it opens on an external stone gallery, which is carried round the tower; it is about one hundred and twenty feet high. Every traveler should ascend this tower, as from its gallery is obtained a most interesting view of the plain; at our feet are the orchards and olive-groves of Ramleh; on the northeast they are touched by those of Sydda, which is seen seated on a gentle eminence beyond; north and south the eye wanders over a boundless plain tinted, according to the season, with the verdure of spring, the golden hue of early summer, or the unvarying gray of autumn; on the west is the sea, and on the east the mountains of Israel. In the plain itself there are but few villages, as it affords too fair a field for Bedouin cavaliers; but the low hills and mountain-sides beyond are thickly studded with villages. We now leave Ramleh for Jerusalem, passing a great many towns; we went into the Jaffa gate, and put up at the Hotel Mediterranean, kept by Houlstein, an Englishman, whose wife is a Scotchwoman.

JERUSALEM.

September 22, 1873.—The great interest attached to Jerusalem is connected with its historical associations; there is little in the character of its antiquities, or in its situation, or in its present state to attract attention, but when viewed in the light of sacred history it is the most interesting spot on earth. Rightly to appreciate it, therefore, we must know its history; every hill and vale, every fountain and grove, and almost every grot and stone has its story. Ten feet from the hotel stood David's

Tower, more than three thousand years old; next to the hotel was Solomon's Pools, and also the Pool of Bethesda, a tank within the Jaffa gate, opposite to King David's Tower; it gets its name from the tradition that King David lived in the Tower of Hippicus, and had thus an opportunity of seeing the too fair wife of the unfortunate Uriah bathing in this pool. I will here mention some of the places I visited in Jerusalem and outside the walls. The Holy Sepulchre, Armenian convent, Caiphas's House, Mount Zion, House of the Lepers, the Tombs of David, Solomon, and Stephen, the Pool of Siloam, the Tomb of Zacharias, the Tomb of Absalom, the place where Isaiah was sawn asunder, the Garden of Gethsemane, the Mount of Olives, the Grotto of Jeremiah, the Pool of Jeremiah, the Valley of Gihon, Jaffa Gate, Damascus Gate, St. Stephen's Gate, Zion Gate, the Golden Gate of the Temple, Aceldama, or field of blood, the Hill of Evil Counsel, Jacob's Well, the lower Pool of Gihon, the Valley of Hinnom, Mount of Offense, Mount Scopus, the Pool of Hezekiah, Mosque Alaxer, the Study of Amar, the Wailing Place of the Jews, Via Dolorosa or Way of Grief, the Tower of Antonius, the entrance gate to Pilate's House, the Tombs of the Kings, the Tombs of the Judges, the Tombs of Helena, Calvary, where Christ ascended, the Mosque of Omar, on the spot where the Temple of Solomon stood.

Jerusalem is one of the greatest cities I have ever seen. The population has been variously estimated at from sixteen thousand to forty thousand, —Moslems, Jews, Greeks, Latins, etc.

RACHEL'S TOMB.

We leave Jerusalem on September 28, 1873, for the convent Mar Saba; here we come to Rachel's Tomb, surmounted by a dome. Rachel died and was buried near Bethlehem; the pillar of Jacob stood over the grave of his beloved wife for a long time.

SOLOMON'S POOLS.

Bethlehem is in sight; we next come to Solomon's Pools; on descending we find that they are partly excavated in the rocky bed of the valley, and built of large hewn stones; they are so arranged that the bottom of the upper pool is higher than the top of the next, and so with the second and third, the object evidently being to collect as great a quantity of water as possible.

BETHLEHEM.

We now make our way to Bethlehem. The sacred interest of this village, though it be little among the thousands of Judea, is only second to Jerusalem itself. The place is first mentioned in connection with the touching narrative of Rachel's death; the next interesting event recorded in the history of the village is when Ruth, the Moabitess, returned with her mother-in-law, Naomi, and gleaned barley in the fields of her husband's kinsman, Boaz; it was to the house of Jesse the Bethlehemite Samuel came, according to the command of the Lord, with his horn of oil, to anoint David, then keeping his father's sheep in the neighboring desert, king over Israel; it was also the city of David. Bethlehem was for a time in the hands of the Philistines, when David and his men were in the Cave of Adullam, and it was then he strangely longed for the waters of Bethlehem, which is by the gate; but that which gave to this little village the first rank among the holiest spots on earth was the birth of the Saviour, born in a stable, and cradled in a manger; here he was seen by the shepherds, who had just heard in the adjoining fields hosts of angels celebrating the praise of the new-born King; here the Eastern Magi worshiped him, and presented their costly gifts. The present inhabitants are said to number about three thousand, and are all Christians; there was formerly a Mohammedan quarter, but after a rebellion of the people in 1834 it was entirely destroyed, by order of Ibrahim Pacha. The inhabitants are peasants, living by cultivation of their fields and gardens, and a few of them spend their spare time in carving beads, crucifixes, models of the Holy Sepulchre, etc., in olive-wood and mother-of-pearl for pilgrims and travelers. The ladies of Bethlehem are celebrated for their beauty, which has something of a European cast, and historians say they are also celebrated for their virtue.

CONVENT.

We left Bethlehem about one o'clock, and arrived at the convent Mar Saba about four o'clock. In the wild grandeur of its situation Mar Saba is the most extraordinary building in Palestine; just at the place where it stands, a small ravine slopes down into Kedron, and the buildings cover both sides of the former and the projecting cliff between the two; the irregular masses of walls, towers, chambers, and chapels here perched up on narrow rock terraces and there clinging to the sides of precipices. The church, an edifice with enormous buttresses, a large dome, and small clock-turret, occupies the point of the rock, and the other buildings are so dispersed along the side from the summit to the bottom of the ravine, that it is impossible to tell how much is masonry and how much nature. Here were sixty-four monks; they never eat any meat, and never admit any women within their gates under any stress of weather or other accident; the monks employ some of their leisure time in feeding and tending flocks of gay, cheerful birds peculiar to this region.

DEAD SEA.

We left Mar Saba for the Dead Sea, Jordan, and Jericho. Here is the Dead Sea. The region is represented as a deep valley, distinguished from the surrounding desert by its fertile fields. There was a man murdered near the sea, and another stabbed last week.

JORDAN.

From here we went to Jordan, about five miles from the sea, and took lunch. The Biblical account corresponds entirely with what we find to be the case at the present day; the Israelites crossed the Jordan four days before the Passover. But another event of still more thrilling interest has been long fixed near this spot: the baptism of our Saviour. All we know is, John came preaching in the wilderness of Judea, and Jesus came from Galilee to Jordan unto John to be baptized of him; it would seem from this that the baptism took place where John baptized many. Mustapha H. Mussa, our dragoman, lives at Alexandria; he said his wife was a Christian, he was an Arab; he wanted A. F. Shanafelt, my companion, to baptize him when yet in Egypt; and now A. F. Shanafelt baptized him in the river Jordan, where John baptized our Saviour.

JERICHO.

From this place we went to Jericho, about ten miles; there stayed over night.

BETHANY.

Next morning we started for Bethany. This is the little hamlet which derives an undying interest from having been the home of our Saviour during his visits to Jerusalem, and from having been the scene of some of the most affecting incidents in his life. What Capernaum was in Galilee, Bethany was in Judea; here he was wont to retire in the quiet evening, after each day of thankless but unceasing toil in the city; here dwelt the sisters Mary and Martha, with Lazarus, their brother, on the father's side. In that deep Valley of Jordan, away among those mountains, Christ was abiding, when the sisters sent to inform him that Lazarus was sick; down that long, dreary desert they often looked in expectation of his coming; on the old road without the village Martha met him with despairing, almost reproachful words, " Lord, if thou hadst been here, my brother had not died;" here he raised Lazarus from his tomb, and presented him to his weeping sisters; here, too, was the house of Simon the Leper, in which the grateful Mary anointed Jesus with precious ointment, and wiped his feet with her hair. The precious sites of these events are still pointed out: the house of Simon, that of Mary and Martha, and the tomb of Lazarus; the latter is a deep vault, partly excavated in the rock, lined with masonry; the entrance is low, and a long, winding, half-ruinous staircase leads down to a small chamber, and from this a few steps more lead down to another smaller vault in which the body is supposed to have lain. The situation of the tomb in the centre of the village scarcely agrees with the Gospel narrative, and the masonry of the interior has no appearance of antiquity, but the real tomb could not have been far distant, and in such a place as this few will think of traditional sites when the unwavering features of nature, the rocks, the glens, the everlasting hills are before them. Some may inquire for the site of Bethpage, but of it no trace, as yet, has been certainly discovered; it appears to me, from the way the two names are used in the Gospel, that they were probably applied to different quarters of the same village: the one called Bethpage, house of figs, from the fig-orchards adjoining it, the other Bethany, house of dates, from its palm-trees. We now proceeded to the Mount of Olives, two miles; it rises two hundred and twenty feet above Moriah, and, being only a half-mile distant, it affords one of the most commanding and interesting views of Jerusalem and its environs.

NABULUS.

We encamped at Mount Olive over night, and next morning started for Nabulus Schaekem. This is the usual route taken by travelers on leaving the Holy City, and is the best, as it leads to some of the most interesting places in Palestine. A sharp lookout must be kept on the plain of Sharon for stray Arab horsemen, who are addicted to raids in that region. So far as natural scenery is concerned, the situation of Nabulus is the finest in

Palestine. In fact, it is the only really beautiful site from Dan to Beersheba. A verdant valley, sparkling with fountains and streams of water, opens from the plain of Mulchna. It is about two hundred feet wide, and is shut in on the north and south by dark, rocky sides of Ebal and Gherizim, which rise sleepily from its bed. Nabulus has a population of about eight thousand, of whom five hundred are Christians, one hundred and fifty Samaritans, and about one hundred and fifty are Jews. The houses are stone, resembling in style and general appearance those of Jerusalem. The chief productions are soap, cotton, and oil. The soap-works are large and the trade is flourishing. The history of this place extends over a period of nearly four thousand years.

JACOB'S WELL.

Jacob's well is a pleasant walk of half an hour down the valley, and we visited it. Next is Jacob's Tomb, in the centre of the valley's mouth. A short distance north of Jacob's Well is a little square area, inclosed by a white wall and having a common Moslem tomb placed diagonally across the floor. This is the traditional tomb of Joseph.

The situation of the ancient royal city of Samaria, or Sebaste, now the village of Sebustieh, if less beautiful, is more commanding than that of Nabulus. Nearly in the centre of a basin, about five miles in diameter, rises a flattish, oval-shaped hill to the height of some three hundred feet. On the summit is a long table-land, which breaks down at the sides, one hundred feet or more, to an irregular terrace or belt of lowland. Below this the roots of the hill spread off more gradually into the surrounding valleys. The modern village of Sebustieh may contain about sixty houses, with a population of four hundred.

NAZARETH.

Here we encamped one night, then made our way to Nazareth, passing a good many towns. The situation of Nazareth is peculiar, but it cannot be called either fine or picturesque. High up among the hills that bound the plain of Esdrelon is a little valley, one mile long from east to west, and one-fourth broad. It is filled with cornfields, and has patches of garden, inclosed by hedges of cactus, sprinkled in clumps and singly here and there through it, and the white limestone of which the walls are composed is dotted and streaked with the foliage of fig-trees, wild shrubs, and little patches of grain. The hills on the north overtop the others, rising to some four hundred feet. The population of Nazareth is thirty-five hundred, or perhaps four thousand, inhabitants. On the eastern side of the village is the fountain of the Virgin, and here the Greeks have their Church of the Annunciation, whose authenticity is grounded on a tradition of older date than that of the Latin Proterangelion.

We are told that the angel came to Mary when she was drawing water from the fountain. The fountain is here still, bearing her name, and over it stands the Greek church, a low, plain building.

TIBERIAS.

Here we stayed over night, and in the morning we left Nazareth for Tiberias, once a splendid city, but now in ruins. It contains about three thousand inhabitants. The ruins of the ancient city are scattered along the shore to the southward, extending as far as the hot baths. Here I took a bath in the hot spring mixed with sulphur. The ruins consist of heaps of stones, foundations of the wall close to the water, and a few dozens of granite columns strewn about. Not a building remains. The very foundations of palaces and temples have disappeared, and the greater part of their materials has been carried off to the modern towns. It is said that at the time of the great earthquake of 1837, and for some days afterwards, the quantity of water issuing from the springs was immensely increased and the temperature much higher than ordinary. Almost every spot along the shore of the Sea of Galilee is holy ground. A great part of our Lord's public life was spent here. After his townsmen at Nazareth rejected and sought to kill him, he came down from the hilly country of Galilee and took up his abode on these shores. But the shores were not then silent and desolate as they are now.

They were teeming with life. The new capital of Galilee had recently been built by Herod Antipas. Many towns, such as Magdala, Capernaum, Chorazin, and the Bethesdas, Gamala, Hippas, and Haricher, stood upon the beach. Other and larger cities, such as Scythopolis, Gadara, and Pella, with numerous populous villages, studded the surrounding country. In no other part of Palestine could our Lord have found such a sphere for his works and words of mercy. After our Lord had been rejected by his own townsmen of Nazareth, he came and dwelt at Capernaum, which was thence called his own city. Here he healed the domestic in the synagogue, cured Peter's mother-in-law, restored the paralytic, called Matthew, cured the centurion's servant, raised Jarius's daughter from the dead, and miraculously obtained the tribute-money from the mouth of a fish near Capernaum. He chose his twelve apostles, delivered his sermon on the mount, spoke the parable of the sowers and tares and the treasure hid in a field, the merchant seeking goodly pearls, and the net cast into the sea. In Capernaum he gave a lecture on fasting, at Levi's feast, on formality to the hypocritical Pharisees, on faith to the people in the synagogue, and on humanity and forbearance and brotherly love to his disciples. Magdala is the place of birth of Mary Magdalene, out of whom Jesus had cast seven devils, and to whom he appeared immediately after his resurrection. The name and site of the village will call up that solemn scene related in John. The swine were forced down into the Sea of Galilee, and were drowned. Here we stayed one night, then went on to the hill of the Judge,— the Dan of Scripture. Two things are here worthy of special notice: the Fountain of Jordan and the site of the ancient city. A cup-shaped dell, sprinkled with trees and covered with a jungle of bushes and rank weeds, stands in the middle of the plain; the southern rim of the dell has an elevation of eighty feet above the plain, and the diameter of the cup may be about one-half mile; at the western base the waters of the great fountain burst out, first forming a miniature lake, and then rushing off a rapid river, southward; it is probably the largest fountain in Syria, but for grandeur and picturesque beauty it cannot be compared to the Fountain of the Abana, at Fijeh. Another smaller fountain springs up within the dell, and flows off through a break in the rim on the southwest; just at this break stands a noble oak-tree, beneath which the traveler will enjoy an hour's rest after the long and dreary ride. Perhaps, too, he may be lulled to sleep by the murmur of waters and the voice of the turtle. Some Moslem saint has found a last resting-place under the shadow of the tree, and his tomb is garlanded with as many old rags as would deck a dozen dervishes. The waters of the two fountains soon unite and wind down the rich plain, both fountain and stream bearing the name of Dan.

SAFED.

The only attraction of Safed is in the splendid view it commands, and the first-visit of the traveler will therefore be to the summit of the castle. It is surrounded by a dry ditch, within which was a wall; all is now a mass of ruins, only a shattered fragment of one of the great round towers having survived the earthquake of 1837 ; before that catastrophe, it was not in the best repair, still it afforded accommodation to the governor and his train. By the earthquake, in a few minutes it was utterly ruined, and many of its inmates buried beneath the fallen towers. The 1st of January, 1837, was indeed a day of horror and woe to Safed; tremendous shocks made the whole hill tremble, more than three-fourths of the houses were prostrated, and nearly five thousand of the inhabitants killed. The Jews suffered most; the houses, huddled together and clinging to the steep declivity, were dashed down by the first shock, those above falling on those below, thus heaping ruin upon ruin. It was estimated that five thousand of them perished; many were killed instantaneously by the falling houses, others engulfed, and died a miserable death before they could be dug out; some were extricated after five or six days, covered with wounds and bruises, fainting with hunger and thirst, and only able to take a last look at the little remnants of their brethren ere they died. The rents are still shown in the earth, made by the earthquake. Here is the deep basin of the Sea of Tiberias, lying nearly two thousand five hundred feet below us, and the rounded top of Taber Cesærea Philippi. Banias is the great fountain, the upper source of the Jordan. A cliff of ruddy limestone, nearly one hundred feet high, rises on the north side of the ruins; at its base is a cave, its mouth incumbered by a heap of débris partly composed of broken fragments of rock, and partly of ancient buildings. The Castle of Subeibeh, generally known as the castle of Banias, is one of the finest ruins in Syria, and one of the most perfect and imposing specimens of the military architecture of the Phœnicians, or, possibly, of the Syro-Grecians extant; it is an hour's ride from Banias; its elevation is at least one thousand feet high above the tower, and, as viewed from the west, it seems to crown a conical peak, but on reaching the summit we find that this peak resolves into a narrow ridge connected with the mountain chain behind, but having a wide chasm on the north, called Wady Ruichabeh, eight hundred feet deep, and another on the south side, wider, but of equal depth. The castle thus occupies a rocky crest which forms the culminating point of the ridge; the only practicable approach to it is on the east, and there a narrow zigzag path leads up the steep bank, among the huge fragments of rock, and then winds along the foot of the ramparts to a small portalice around the tower, near the southwestern angle. The building occupies an area about one thousand feet long by two hundred in its greatest breadth, shaped something like the figure 8, narrow in the centre, and bulging out at each end; the interior is uneven. The natural rock rises in places higher than the walls; immense cisterns are hewn in it, which contain an abundant supply of water. Many of the stones in the walls are eight, ten, and twelve feet long, carefully dressed and beveled. From here we made our way to Kehr Hauwar, October 2, 1873.

KEHR HAUWAR.

Kehr Hauwar is a large, prosperous village, surrounded by gardens, orchards, and fruitful fields, and inhabited partly by Druized and partly by Moslems.

Tradition has placed here one of the numerous tombs of Nimrod. Many of the houses are in ruins in this town. From here we traveled to Damascus, passing many towns on the way.

DAMASCUS.

Damascus, October 3, 1873.—The population of this city is estimated at one hundred and seventy-five thousand; of these about twenty thousand are Christians, eight thousand Jews, and the rest

Mohammedans. From recent very careful statistics, it appears that before the massacre of 1860 the Christian population numbered nearly thirty-four thousand; at present, it is under twenty thousand. The Christian quarter of the city, which lays near the east gate, on both sides of the street called Straight, was plundered and burned to ashes; not a single house was left. After the massacre of Damascus, the clergy and chief people of each sect made out, so far as the names could be ascertained, lists of the persons belonging to their community who were killed; these lists contained the names of about two thousand five hundred known inhabitants of the city; it is certain, therefore, that that number at least of persons permanently resident in Damascus perished during the three days of the massacre. I am persuaded, therefore, that we are rather below than above the truth in saying that on the 9th, 10th, and 11th of July, 1860, there were murdered in Damascus at least two thousand five hundred adult male Christians. The bazaars of Damascus have long been celebrated, and they are among the best in the East. Long ranges of stalls are on each side of narrow covered lanes, with a bearded, turbaned, robed figure squatting in a corner of each, as composedly as if he had been placed there for a show, like the piles of silk that rise up on each side of him. Each trade has its own quarter or section in the immense network of bazaars, and thus we run in succession through the mercer's bazaar, the tailor's bazaar, the spice bazaar, the tobacco bazaar, the shoe bazaar, the silversmith's bazaar, the saddler's bazaar, and the "old Clo" bazaar. The bazaars are all well stocked with India muslin, Manchester prints, Persian carpets, Lyons silk, Damascus swords, Birmingham knives, amber mouth-pieces, antique chinaware, cashmere shawls, French ribbons, Mocha coffee, and Dutch sugar all mingled together. Those who have a taste for curiosities, such as old arms, porcelain, etc., ought to visit the Greek bazaar near the gate of the palace; but be it remembered that five or six times the value of each article is usually asked. Some of the principal places of interest in Damascus are the Armenian Convent, Greek, Catholic, and Syrian Churches, house of Ananias, Lazarist Convent, Latin Convent, and Khan Assad Pasha; the house of Judas is still standing, in a good state of preservation; British Consulate, Custom-House, Tomb of Sidy Balal, Tomb of St. George, Bab Kisan, where Paul was let down from the wall, together with the scene of Paul's conversion, the Leper's Hospital, the house of Naaman, and many other valuable sights. We stayed at Damascus two nights.

BEYROUT.

We then started for Beyrout, on the Mediterranean Sea, which is a city of ten thousand inhabitants, finely situated on the sea. The vessels have no wharf at this city, and so it is at all the cities in Egypt and Syria. They have to anchor out in the sea two or three hundred yards. Here the bankers would not give us any money on Jay Cooke & Co.'s circular letter of credit, Philadelphia, May 30, 1873, on account of Jay Cooke & Co. failing in Philadelphia. I tried them several times, but they would do nothing. I went to the American Consul; he thought he could do nothing, but said, come back to-morrow, and I will see what I can do. I went back, and finally he agreed to give me enough money to take me to London.

TYRE—HIRAM.

So I got the money, and we made out to get on a steamer on the 10th of October, 1873, which will sail by Tyre, where Hiram was buried, and Jaffa; they say it will stay at Jaffa half or three-quarters of a day; from thence to Port Said, stopping there; thence to Alexandria, where we land, and then take a steamboat for Marseilles, in the southern part of France; from there we take the cars for Paris, five hundred miles; from there to London; from there to Liverpool, where we will take a steamer for New York, perhaps on the 11th of November, 1873, after which I hope to reach New York in safety.

NEW YORK.

November 25, 1873.—My dear and loving wife:

I want you to come to Philadelphia on the eleven o'clock A.M. train, on the 26th of November. I will be at the depot when the train arrives if I am not detained in any way; wait half an hour, and if not there go to the Bingham House, Market Street. I will be there if nothing happens me seriously. Come down, my dear wife. Good-by.

Yours very affectionately,

JOHN VANDERSLICE.

The following appeared in the "Independent Phœnix," of Phœnixville, in September, 1874:

"DEVIL'S INK.

"We were shown a letter, written by our townsman John Vanderslice, Esq., from the Geyser Springs, in California, with the Devil's Ink. This fluid gushes forth from the interior of the earth, and is as black as his satanic majesty is supposed to be. The ink appears on paper to be equal to Hover's or Thad. Davis's celebrated ink.

"THE TOURIST.

"Our townsman, Mr. John Vanderslice, again started on a tour through foreign countries around the world, and as his many friends are interested in knowing his objective points, we give a brief synopsis of his proposed route, taken under the guidance of Cook, Son & Jenkins, the New York excursion agency.

"Mr. Vanderslice will join the excursion party at

Chicago, October 1 ; thence they journey by easy stages, stopping at all prominent points, to Omaha, Salt Lake City, and San Francisco; there they take a steamer for Yokohama, about the 10th of November. From Yokohama they voyage to the inland sea of Japan, arriving at Shanghai in about seven days' time; thence they go to Hongkong, make a short trip to Canton, and leave Hongkong so as to reach Singapore on the 16th of December. From Singapore they go through the Straits of Malacca to Penang; thence to Point-de-Galli, Ceylon; they expect to leave Ceylon on the 2d of January, 1875, so as to arrive at Calcutta about the 11th of the month, calling at Madras on the way, if the surf, as it frequently happens, is not so heavy as to prevent a landing. From Calcutta they go to Benares, the Holy City of the Hindoos, by railroad; the next point is Agra, and from there they go to Delhi; thence to Cawnpore and Lucknow; from Lucknow they go to Allahabad, Jubbulpore, and Bombay. In Bombay they will spend six days, and then journey on to Aden and Suez, arriving at the latter place February 8. Thence they are carried by rail to Cairo, where they take boats, and go up the sacred Nile some five hundred miles. Returning to Cairo, they go thence to Alexandria, in Egypt; thence to Brendecia; thence to Naples; a stop of two days is made in Naples, and then to Rome; and then they go to

Florence and Turin. At Turin they take an express train for Paris, where a week will be passed amid the festivities of the gay French capital. Thence they go to London, and thence to Liverpool, where they take a steamer for New York. The time that will be consumed in the trip will be about six months."

"FOREIGN TOUR.

"We learn that John Vanderslice, of Phœnixville, will go out upon his trip on one of Cook, Son & Jenkins' 'Educational Tours.' This company is located at 261 Broadway, New York, and do an immense business as tourists and excursion managers. They are general agents for passenger traffic on all the principal railways, steamboats, and diligence companies throughout the world, and to sail from America with one of their tickets for a tour around the world in one's pocket is to save much time and annoyance. We doubt not, Jules Verne could have sent Phineas Fogg around the world in seventy-five days, had he patronized Cook, Son & Jenkins."

CHICAGO.

I left Phœnixville September 29, 1874, arriving at Chicago on the 30th of September; stayed two days at the Sherman House. I was in Chicago in 1871, just before the great fire broke out; it was then a fine city, containing some of the finest storehouses I ever saw in any place, and the finest hotels, perhaps, in the world; but the fire destroyed the greater part of the city.

Chicago is nine hundred and sixty-three miles from Philadelphia, and has within thirty years grown from a small Indian trading post to the position of the Metropolis of the Northwest, and is now the greatest railway centre on the continent. It is situated on the western shore of Lake Michigan, at the mouth of the Chicago River. By means of the latter and the Illinois and Michigan Canal it has continuous communication with the Mississippi River and the Gulf of Mexico on the south and west, and with the chain of the great lakes, the St. Lawrence, and the Atlantic. No city in the world possesses greater facilities for commercial intercourse. At the close of 1830, Chicago contained twelve houses and three suburban (country) residences on Madison Street, with a population, composed of whites, half-breeds, and blacks, numbering about one hundred. The first map of the town, as surveyed by James Thompson, bears date August 4, 1830. The town was organized August 10, 1833, incorporated as a city March 4, 1837, and the first election held May 1, 1837. The first vessel entered the harbor June 11, 1834, and by the official census taken July 1, 1837, the entire population was found to be four thousand one hundred and eighty. The first frame building was erected, in 1832, by George W. Dale, and the first brick house in 1833; the latter was standing on Monroe Street, near Clark, at a recent period. In 1843 the population of the city had increased to 7580, in 1848 to 16,859, in 1850 to 28,269, in 1855 to 80,023, in 1860 to 109,263, and in 1865 to 188,539; its present population, city and suburban, is more than 450,000. During the years 1856-58 the entire business portion of the city was raised from three to eight feet above its former level, which has facilitated drainage, and greatly improved its sanitary condition as well as the commercial facilities. I was at Chicago at the time it was raised; the merchants selling goods in entire blocks of buildings that were raised, four, five, and six stories high, without much cracking in the ceilings, or interruption to business. In Chicago itself, there had been several unusually destructive fires on previous days, tiring the firemen and disorganizing the department, and finally, on the evening of Sunday, the 8th of October, 1871, the main conflagration commenced, having its origin in a small wooden barn on DeHaven street, in the western district of the city. The total area burned over in the city, including streets, was very nearly three and one-third square miles; the number of buildings destroyed, seventeen thousand four hundred and fifty, and the number of persons rendered homeless was ninety-eight thousand five hundred; of the latter, upwards of two hundred and fifty are said to have lost their lives. Including depreciation in real estate and loss of business, occasioned by the fire, the grand total of pecuniary damage has been estimated at two hundred and ninety million dollars; there was insurance on this to the amount of one hundred million dollars, of which hardly one-half could be collected, the first result of the fire being to bankrupt many of the insurance companies all over the country. Of the old court-house, an immense structure which occupied a square in the centre of the city, nothing is left but a portion of the fire-blackened walls. It is not yet built up. There has been another very destructive fire this year (1874). I visited the whole ruins; there are thousands of buildings laying in ruins, including a great many churches and public buildings; some of them are now being rebuilt. The Douglas Monument at Chicago occupies a site formerly owned by Mr. Douglas himself; the tract, one acre in extent, was purchased from Mr. Douglas for the sum of thirty thousand dollars. The monument consists of a circular base, fifty-two feet in diameter; a pedestal, twenty-one feet high, and column of forty-three feet, surmounted by a sphere upon which a bronze statue of Douglas, twelve feet high, is to be placed; the entire height of the monument when completed will be one hundred feet, and the cost seventy-five thousand dollars.

COUNCIL BLUFFS.

From here we made our way to Council Bluffs, the capital of Potawatamie County, Iowa.

It is situated in the Missouri bottom, at the foot of the bluffs, which are here high and very precipitous. The river seems to vibrate between the bluffs, eating the earth away from the one side, and depositing it upon the other, so that this city, which, when first settled, was upon the river's edge, is now three miles away from it. This gives it plenty of room to extend its limits, and it is probable that however it may increase its population, there will always be room for manufacturing establishments, while upon the bluffs, at no distant day, will be clustered residences, elegant churches, pleasure-grounds, and other accessories of a large city. The views from these bluffs are very beautiful. In 1804 Clark and Lewis held a council here with the Indians, and gave it its name. The streets cross each other at right angles, one set running from the river to the bluffs, which stay their further progress in that direction. There is an expensive court-house at this place, and the State Institute for the Deaf and Dumb, now building, will be an ornament to the city.

OMAHA.

Here we make our way across the bridge to Omaha. I was here in 1855; there were then only six frame shanties in this place; now, Omaha is the principal city between Chicago and the Pacific, and is destined to be one of the largest in the West. The site is a plateau rising from the river westward to the bluffs, and the city presents a fine appearance to the traveler crossing the wide Mississippi Valley from the eastward. The hills on the west command a splendid view of Council Bluffs; on the east the wide Missouri River, for miles north and south, and an extensive undulating prairie, covered with rich farms, on the west. The situation of Omaha, commanding for it an extensive trade with the west, has caused its almost unprecedented growth from a population of one thousand eight hundred and thirty-three in 1860, to that of eighteen thousand, shown by the late census. There are a number of first-class hotels, but to meet the wants of the public at this great central point of the continent, a handsome five-story hotel was erected recently at a cost of two hundred thousand dollars.

The bridge at this point across the Missouri, one of the finest structures of the kind in the country, is finished, and affords unbroken railway connection from ocean to ocean. It was built by the Union Pacific Company, and cost over one million dollars. It is a magnificent structure of iron, sixty feet above high-water mark, and has, beside a railroad track, a street-car and wagon way. There are in Omaha seventeen church edifices, some of which are very handsome. The high-school house, in course of erection, at a cost of two hundred thousand dollars, and the brick buildings recently erected in the different parts of the city for graded schools, are all of the first order.

From Omaha we commenced our journey on the Union Pacific Railway, nine in number; we were seated in one of the luxurious Pullman palace cars, with which every American or foreign traveler is familiar. Passing the wooded hills, a wide, rolling prairie opens before us, with fine farmhouses, and groves and timber about them; on the left is the belt of forest along the bluffs of the Missouri River, and we can hardly realize that only a few years ago this country was inhabited by the red men, and that the tread of the pioneers had not been heard west of the great tributary of the Father of Waters.

SHERMAN.

We make our way to Sherman Bay (five hundred and forty-nine miles, elevation eight thousand two hundred and thirty-five feet), the most elevated railroad station in the world, and possessing many attractions for the tourist. Those wishing for clear mountain air, fine trout-fishing, and a wide field for botanical study, will find them here. We push for the Devil's Gate Station, Utah Territory, where the road is again between high rocks and lofty mountains. Just below the station is Devil's Gate, where the stream rushes through a narrow gorge. If the tourist can stop for a view of this wild scene, and climb to the top of the high knoll on the right, he will look down on a rush of waters sixty feet below him with a loud roar like that of a cataract, while the wall on the opposite side rises up to a great height. Passing over a bridge high above the stream now escaped from its confinement, he can look down on its foaming waters as they dash against the big boulders in the channel. Three miles farther we emerge from the grim battlements of rocks and catch the first view of Salt Lake Valley,—Ogden, Utah Territory. Supposing that every person traveling for pleasure will wish to see the desert home of the Mormons, we shall here leave the main road and, after a ride of forty miles in the cars of the Utah Central Railway, find ourselves at Salt Lake City.

SALT LAKE.

Salt Lake City, October 5, 1874.—Put up at the Revere House, Main Street, D. R. Patton & Co., proprietors. The capital of the Territory of Utah is ten hundred and sixty-eight miles west of Omaha and nine hundred and sixteen miles east of San Francisco. It lies in the valley, extending close up to the base of the Wasatch Mountains, on the north, with an expansive view on the south of more than one hundred miles of plains, beyond which in the distance rise clear and grand in the extreme the gray jagged and ragged mountains, whose peaks are covered with perpetual snow. The highest of these mountains is eleven thousand four hundred feet above the sea. The population of Salt Lake City by the last census is eighteen thousand seven hundred and twenty, those born in the United States numbering ten thousand two hundred and fourteen, and in other countries seven thousand and sixty-eight. This at first glance seems to contradict the popular belief that the followers of Brigham Young have been recruited chiefly in foreign countries, but when the tables showing the nativity of parents, the relative number of the sexes, and the number of children are prepared, this seeming contradiction may be explained. The city covers an area of about nine miles, or three miles each way, and is handsomely laid out; the streets are very wide, with irrigating ditches passing through all of them, keeping the shade-trees and orchards in beautiful order. Every block is surrounded with shade-trees, and nearly every house has its neat little orchard of apple-, peach-, apricot-, plum-, and cherry-trees. Fruit is very abundant; and the almond, the catalpa, and the buttonwood-trees grow side by side with the maple, the willow, and the locust,—in fact, the whole nine square miles is almost one continuous garden. From the Ensign Park one of the finest views of the overland line is obtained. The city is divided into blocks of ten acres, each block being divided into eight lots: these are only subdivided in the business and more thickly settled parts of the city. The blocks are divided into wards, of which there are twenty, each having its meeting-house and bishop. The building material mostly used is sun-dried brick covered with plaster, and the houses are generally of one story, covering much space. A few of the houses on newer streets are built of stone, and are elegant within and without. There are three hotels—the Salt Lake, Towndson, and Revere House. We put up at the Revere House, one of the latest built, which is a first-rate hotel. There are several small boarding-houses and restaurants. The theatre—the chief place of entertainment—is a great building, gloomy-looking from the street, but the interior is handsomely finished in white and gold. It is one hundred and seventy-two feet long, eighty feet wide, and forty feet from floor to ceiling. It seats sixteen hundred persons, and in its arrangements and appointments is considered the finest on the continent outside of New York City. There are several public halls where concerts and other entertainments are given; but the chief amusement of the Mormons is dancing, and this is done principally in the school-houses or meeting-houses. The Tabernacle is the first object to attract the eye as one approaches the city, although far removed from being imposing or possessing any architectural beauty. It is built of wood, excepting the forty-six parallelogram pillars of red sandstone upon which rests its immense dome-like roof; these pillars are nine feet deep by three feet wide, and about twelve feet high, the space between them being filled up with doors and windows.

The Tabernacle is the largest hall on the continent with a single-span self-supporting roof; it is oval in shape inside and out, two hundred and fifty feet long and one hundred and fifty feet wide, and will seat comfortably from thirteen thousand to fifteen thousand persons; the ceiling is sixty-two feet from the floor; the place is used for worship, lectures, and debates The Tabernacle organ is the largest ever built in the United States; there are only two larger in the country, both of which were brought from Europe. The Mormon organ has two thousand pipes; it was built by an Englishman, Mr. Joseph Ridges; the wood-work is white mountain pine, stained a dark mahogany-color. Brigham's Block, which is east of Temple Block, contains the Tithing-house, "Deseret News" office, Brigham's Beehive-house, the Lion-house, his private telegraph-office, and other offices, the museum, a private school-house, and various other smaller buildings, dwellings, shops, etc., the whole inclosed by a solid, high stone wall, with close, heavy gates.

GREAT SALT LAKE.

The Great Salt Lake is so salty that no living thing can exist in it. The road skirts the north side of the lake, while the Mormon city lies east of the south end of it. It is about forty-five miles in width, and one hundred and twenty-six miles long; as quiet and placid amid its mountain barriers as the water in a basin. It has numerous islands on its bosom, one of which, called Antelope, is fifteen miles in length. The water of this lake is so buoyant that it is difficult to sink in it, and if allowed to dry on one's body the salt will fall off in scales. Those islands would make magnificent summer resorts, and probably the day is not very far distant when they will be occupied for that purpose, and little pleasure-steamers will be used to explore their recesses. After leaving the promontory and borders of Salt Lake, we enter upon that extended plateau, about sixty miles in width and the same in length, known as the Great American Desert, which extends over an area of about sixty square miles, stopping at Sacramento. We there took dinner, and from there proceeded to San Francisco.

SAN FRANCISCO.

San Francisco, October 25, 1874.—This large and flourishing city, the metropolis of the Pacific coast, is situated on the western side of the bay of San Francisco, and at the north end of a peninsula formed by the Pacific Ocean on the west, and the bay of San Francisco on the east, in latitude 37°, 48 N. The early history of San Francisco is interesting on account of the rapid growth of the place. The first house was built in 1835, when the village was called Yerba Buena (which in Spanish signifies good herb), so named from a medicinal plant growing in abundance in the vicinity. In 1847 this was changed to San Francisco, and in 1848, the year that gold was first discovered in California by the white settlers, the population had grown to one thousand. The influx from the East then commenced, and in December, 1850, the population had grown to twenty-five thousand. From this small beginning it has steadily increased, with some temporary drawbacks, until, in 1860, the population was fifty-six thousand eight hundred and two; in 1870 it reached one hundred and forty-nine thousand four hundred and eighty two; and in 1873 it reached four hundred thousand. As an illustration of the extent of the business of the city, it may be stated that the manufacturing establishments now in operation in San Francisco number upwards of eight hundred, employing a capital of eighteen million dollars, consuming annually material of the value of twenty-three million dollars, and producing goods worth forty-five million dollars. In three months of 1871 San Francisco imported 10,700,304 pounds of rice, 15,936,-

865 pounds of sugar, 2,766,196 pounds of coffee, and 833,472 pounds of tea direct from the Pacific. In 1870 it exported fifteen million pounds of wool. " Other things," says a traveler, " than the increase of population and the enlargement of the city have made the growth of San Francisco an event without a parallel either in America or in any other quarter of the habitable globe. Its name had become synonymous for all that was most shameless in profligacy, for all that was basest in depravity, for all that was wanton and brutal in ruffianism. In the open day men were murdered with impunity; at night the property of the citizens was at the mercy of the lawless. The scum of Polynesia, desperadoes from Australia, bullies and blackguards from the wild State of Missouri, Spanish cut-throats from the cities of the Pacific coast, dissolute women, and reckless adventurers from the slums of Europe congregated in San Francisco, and there plied their several avocations and followed their devious courses in defiance of the prohibitions of a law that had lost its terrors for them, and in disregard of any other check save the revolver or the bowie-knife. At that time San Francisco was one-half a brothel and one-half a gaming hell. There came a crisis in the annals of the city when the action of the law was forcibly impeded in order that the reign of law might be restored. A vigilance committee discharged the

fourfold functions of police, judge, jury, and executioner. A short shrift and lofty gallows was the fate of the criminal whom they took in the act of committing robbery or murder. The remedy was strong and dangerous, but the symptoms were so threatening as to inspire fear lest what man calls civilization should cease to exist, and no peril incurred in applying the remedy was comparable to the risk of allowing the disease to spread and become intensified. Never perhaps in the history of the world did the result more completely justify the means employed than in the case of San Francisco. The committee discharged its duties with unrelenting severity so long as professional thieves and systematic murderers were at large triumphing in their crimes. As soon, however, as order was restored, the vigilance committee decreed its own dissolution, and the dispensers of summary justice became conspicuous for their obedience to administrators of the law. From being a byword for its lawlessness and licentiousness, the city of San Francisco has become in a little more than ten years as moral as Philadelphia, and far more orderly than New York."

We all stopped at the Grand Hotel of San Francisco, Johnson & Co., proprietors, situated on Market Street, corner of New Montgomery. It is built with a view to elegance and comfort. It has a front of two hundred and five feet on Market

Street, and three hundred and thirty-five on New Montgomery Street. The style of decoration is elaborately ornate. The building is three stories in height, and there is a fourth story in the mansard-roof. The rooms are arranged in suites. The Grand Hotel now building on New Montgomery Street is one of the largest in the United States, and perhaps in the world. They make room for thirty-five hundred persons. It belongs to the same company that owns the Grand Hotel. It is exactly opposite the Grand Hotel. The company owns three blocks on both sides of Montgomery Street, and expects to buy the Lick House, which will soon be sold and changed into stores. It has twenty-five hundred hands working on it at this time, and one thousand hands making furniture. The United States Mint (branch) is on the north side of Commercial Street, near Montgomery. Office hours from nine A.M. to two P.M. Gold bullion received from nine A.M. to twelve M., and silver bullion from twelve M. to ten P.M. Visitors admitted from nine A.M. to twelve M. At this establishment is made two-thirds of all the gold and silver coin manufactured in the United States. One hundred men and three coining-presses are kept constantly busy, two hundred and forty-two million dollars having been coined between 1854, the year of its establishment, and 1867, inclusive, —an amount nearly equal to one-half the entire coinage of the Philadelphia Mint since its origin in 1793.

There are probably about thirty thousand Chinese in San Francisco. On every block we see them. At the turn of every corner I see ever present the nankeen pants, turban hat, and pigtail of John. They all dress in about the same style; ragged or patched coats or pants are seldom to be seen. In almost every family or restaurant are to be found the Chinese cooks. In every street you will pass some Chang or Wang sign hung out, with the words " Washing and ironing done here."

THE CHINESE THEATRE.

No person visiting San Francisco should fail to visit the Chinese theatre. It is located in the centre of Chinatown, in the northern part of San Francisco. Here all the Chinese in the city have congregated. They hold undisputed possession of several blocks, and the houses are crammed from cellar and sub-cellar to garret. The theatre is a two-story building, the entrance to the same being through a long, dirty, yellow-papered alley. Every person is smoking, and if the visitor happens to have a seat in the gallery he will have ample opportunity for judging of the difference between the smell of very bad cigars and opium. The stage is about ten feet high, and is covered on all sides with dirty red and yellow paper and black Chinese letters; faded gilt stripes are here and there observable. Pieces of tin like sardine-boxes piled on top of each other are nailed to the wall; wings, tails, and heads of birds are hung up with old tin pans, broken chairs, legless tables, dirty coats, hats, and pants, rusty swords, broomsticks burned black for spears, peacock-feathers, red and yellow strips of muslin, old boots and shoes, wooden animals painted every color but the natural, junks with sails, set armies marching and bulls fighting,—in fact, the stage is indescribable. Imagine all the things in Barnum's Museum thrown out of the windows in an indiscriminate heap, and an idea can be formed of the Chinese theatre. The orchestra sits on the stage, and the musicians smoke all the time. Some have things like horseshoes fastened to a stick a yard long; these they strike together. Others have gongs in their hands, one of which is so large it is fastened to a table, and the fellow who strikes it blows like a blacksmith swinging the sledge-hammer on an anvil. Another has a brass thing like a wash-tub, as high as his head; this he pounds with two things like stilts. There is no music; it is simply each man trying to make more noise than his fellow. After the orchestra have worn themselves out with making the noise, the performance commences. Several fellows clad in green, red, and yellow costumes, with long feathers sticking out from the backs of their necks, wings on their shoulders, and large masks in imitation of bulls, horses, and other beasts, begin strutting about and shouting one to another. It is impossible for any one, except he be a Chinaman, to understand what is going on. Here also can be seen the Chinese ladies sitting in a separate compartment in the gallery. It is quite a common thing to see them here with their opium-pipes, and a little basket containing the tea-pot with tea ready made, and several small cups. While the performance is going on they are alternately drinking tea and smoking opium.

I am going to China on the Colorado on the 31st of October, 1874, with six friends, who are very kind and gentlemanly in every respect.

THE TEMPLES.

The Chinese have three temples at present in San Francisco. The two principal gods are "Hoo Toong" and "Guong Fi." At all hours of the day the visitors will find the temples open, and any number of joss-sticks smoking in front of their favorite gods. We all made a tour to the Cliff House, Seal Rock, Farallone Islands, etc. The favorite drive of the pleasure-seekers of San Francisco is to the Cliff House, which is built on the edge of the cliff at the northern side of the entrance to the Golden Gate. By land it is seven miles from the city. A fine broad macadamized road of five miles in length leads from the outskirts of the city to a group of cliffs outside the Golden Gate to the shore of the Pacific. Seal Rock is close by the hotel, and the greatest charm of the place is the lounge upon the wide, shaded piazza facing the bold rocks, watching the seals, which thrust their heads from the water and cover these rocks, basking in the sun, sleeping, or wriggling their clumsy bodies up and down so noisily that they are heard above the superb roar of the breakers. Northward lies the Golden Gate, through whose entrance sail in and out vessels of all descriptions. The Farallone Islands, a rugged mass of rock of almost two hundred acres in extent, belonging to the Farallone Egg Company, are twenty-five miles from the Cliff House. Here the murre, a large bird, resorts and deposits her eggs. At a distance the birds hovering over the island look like a dark cloud. The whole island is covered with nests. The company robs the nests, and supplies the whole country and city with eggs. Several hundred thousand eggs are gathered every season. So great is the trade that the company has a vessel which in the season makes regular trips between San Francisco and the Farallone Islands.

CALIFORNIA FRUITS AND GRAIN.

California is a wonder. Wonderful alike for the wildness and grandness of her scenery, for the richness of her mines, for the fertility of her soil, and for the salubrity of her climate,—a climate as delightful and healthy as any upon which the sun ever shone, a soil in whose bosom most of the products of the habitable globe find a congenial home, and a country overflowing with the bounties of Providence, where God and nature seem to have set their seal as the garden of the world.

Wheat is the great crop of California. More than one-fourth of the cultivated land is devoted to it. Barley and oats are raised to a considerable extent, but Indian corn was seldom seen in our travels. The annual grain crop is about thirty-two million bushels, two-thirds of which is wheat. In favorable seasons the average yield of wheat is about twenty-five bushels to the acre. In new and very fertile locations it has reached fifty, and even sixty and seventy, bushels per acre.

The supply of culinary vegetables is very abundant, and of excellent quality. When we arrived, on the 20th of June, celery, cauliflowers, and marrow squashes of famous size were in the market. With irrigation successive crops may be obtained, so that you may find anything you desire at any season. The early vegetables begin to come in during the month of February. The size to which they obtain is almost incredible. We were told of pumpkins weighing two hundred and fifty pounds, squashes of one hundred and fifty pounds, beets of one hundred pounds, and carrots of thirty pounds.

Next to the cereals, the grape is the most important. The State has about thirty million vines, two-thirds of which are full-bearing. Many vineyards yield from fifty to five hundred dollars per acre. Some of the varieties, such as the "Flame Tokay," have occasionally yielded eight thousand to ten thousand pounds per acre. Nearly all the vines are foreign varieties, the chief being the Mission, Muscat of Alexandria, the Black Hamburg, and Rose of Peru. The grapes sold for eating bring from four to ten cents per pound, but three-fourths are sold to wine-manufacturers for about twenty dollars a ton. The yield is constant and regular, there being no danger from frost and rain. Vines are grown in tree-form, without stake or trellis, the stems from two to three feet high, and some of the oldest fully six inches in diameter. No summer-pruning is practiced. The bearing canes are allowed to run their full length, spreading over the ground, which is kept clean and well cultivated. They are planted eight feet apart. The cost of cultivation is about twenty-five dollars per acre. The average product is about twelve pounds per vine throughout the State. The Mission frequently yields thirty to forty pounds. Some of the vineyards are from three hundred to five hundred acres in extent. One of the finest visited had an arbor three-quarters of a mile long, thirty feet wide, and twelve feet high. It was used as a drive. The superior advantages of California have destined the State to become one of the greatest grape-growing and wine-producing territories of the earth.

Fruits and trees are in great measure free from insects and disease, but it is reasonable to suppose that those which exist will increase with the advance of fruit-culture, the same as in the older countries. We saw a few caterpillars on the apple, slug on the pear and cherry, aphis on the orange and olive, and mildew on the grape, cracking of the pear and curling of the peach-leaf; but in each instance only in a slight degree. In the valley of Santa Clara we visited a large orchard, which consisted of eight thousand pear-trees, four thousand apple-trees, thirty-five acres of strawberries, ten acres of grapes,—in all, seventy-three acres. Grapes were planted among the pears, the orchard having been planted in 1855. The pear-orchard was composed of many of the leading well-known sorts; the trees were remarkable for health, vigor of growth, and productiveness; the oldest were about twelve years, and some of these we estimated at thirty feet in height and a foot in diameter of trunk at the ground. The apple-orchard was less promising than the pear, we thought, owing to the ground being too wet at a certain period of the year. The strawberry here, when irrigated, bears the whole year, but the principal crops commence in April and continue into September. The plants were six years old, the hills fully of eighteen inches across, and were bearing ripe and green fruit and blossoms at the same time. The owner has three artesian wells on his premises, varying in depth from three hundred and twenty to three hundred and forty feet, giving a constant flow of water during the dry season. The strawberries are irrigated by carrying the water along the headlands in wooden flumes about eighteen inches square; stoppers are inserted opposite the spaces between the rows, and then the water is distributed and shut off at pleasure.

On the 28th of June we visited the plantation of another gentleman at San Lorenzo, who has one hundred and twenty-five acres in fruits, planted fifteen years since, and was one of the earliest, most experienced, and successful fruit-growers in that country. We found him in his extensive and well-arranged fruit-packing house, preparing apricots, cherries, early plums, pears, and currants for market. All were remarkably fine. He had sent that morning to San Francisco cherries that measured three and three-fourths inches in circumference, and counted thirty-six to the pound. He sends annually about sixty-five thousand pounds of cherries, at from ten to forty cents per pound, though some of the earliest had brought seventy-five cents per pound. All are sold in San Francisco; the Black Tartarian always securing the highest price. He has forty acres of cherry-currants. The bushes were covered with masses of fruit of enormous size. He has sold one hundred and forty thousand pounds in one year at from nine to eleven cents per pound. The currants are trained in bush form on single stems, and the branches are carefully shortened during the growing season to keep them compact and prevent breaking down. Of blackberries he has eight or ten acres, all Lawton. Generally this berry does not succeed as well as at the East, though we saw exceptions. Pears are packed in fifty- and apples in sixty-pound boxes. Pears thrive here grandly; and he has raised the pound or Uvedale St. Germain, weighing four pounds three ounces. Almonds are grown to great size both in the tree and fruit. We saw one tree fourteen years old and fifteen inches in diameter that has yielded three bushels, which were sold at twenty-eight cents per pound. He has two thousand trees on his grounds. The English walnut succeeds as well, and some of the trees are already large enough to bear two bushels of nuts each. It may be of interest to put on record some statements of the prices at which these fine fruits were sold. While the growers complain of low prices, the dealers keep them up. We were frequently in the fruit market of San Francisco between the 22d of June and the 19th of July, and find the following notes in our memoranda. It will be understood that these prices are all in gold and silver, and were taken on several different days. Prices vary, of course, from day to day according to the supply and demand. In the latter part of June the prices at wholesale or by the box were: for cherries, ten to thirty-five cents per pound; apricots, eight to ten cents per pound; strawberries, ten to fifteen cents per pound; currants, ten to fifteen cents per pound. July 14 to 19: peaches, fifty cents to one dollar per half-basket; strawberries, three to ten cents per pound; plums, six to twelve cents per pound; currants, ten cents per pound; grapes, fifteen to twenty-five cents per pound; early harvest apples, fifty to seventy-five cents per box; of sixty pounds red Astrachan apples, two to two dollars and fifty cents per box; red June apples, one dollar and fifty cents per box; figs, four to five cents per pound; Royal Ann (Napoleon) cherries, thirty to thirty-five cents per pound; Belle Magnifique cherries, and other varieties, fifteen to twenty cents per pound; Bloodgood pears, two to three dollars per box of fifty pounds; Tyson pears, one dollar and fifty cents per box; Mission pears, one dollar and fifty cents per box; blackberries, ten to fifteen cents per pound; apricots, four to seven cents per pound.

ON THE PACIFIC.

On the 31st of October, 1874, at twelve o'clock noon, we took our traps on board the Colorado, one of the large and splendid ships of the Pacific Mail Steamship Company, plying between San

Francisco and Japan and China. We were booked for a long voyage, not being allowed to see land for twenty-two days, the allotted time which, by the rules of the company, the captain is required to fill out before reaching the port of Yokohama. The Colorado is one of the finest ships of the fleet to which she belongs. She measures four thousand tons, is three hundred and seventy feet in length and seventy-nine in breadth; her depth of hold is thirty-one and a half feet. As we are sailing, she is twenty feet out of water; her cylinder is one hundred and five inches in diameter, and her smoke-pipe is thirty-six feet in circumference,—not a very small chimney. She is registered to carry fourteen hundred and fifty passengers, of which number we had only about forty-seven cabin, nearly all of these Chinese returning to their former homes. The ship carries thirteen large life-boats, all ready for launching, each one capable of floating some fifty persons or more; but it adds very little to my sense of security to see this array of life-boats. In those sudden emergencies which constitute one-half of the chief dangers of the sea, it is seldom that they are successfully launched, or prove of any essential service to the mass of the passengers. The crew, as well as the servants in the cabin and the waiters at the table, are all Chinese, but they are admirably trained, are perfectly quiet, and ready at every call and for any emergency. The fire alarm was sounded soon after leaving port merely to accustom the men to the warning, the passengers having been duly notified, and every man was at his post. The Chinese sailors are born and brought up on the water, many of the families of populous cities living in boats, so that they may be considered a sort of amphibious animal, and they would probably be as strange on land as a fish out of water. We found in Captain Morse a gentlemanly, polite officer, not only looking well to his ship,—the first duty of a seaman,—but attending as well to the comfort and pleasure of his passengers, which cannot be said of all sea-captains. One ship that we expected we did not see; on leaving San Francisco we were informed that we should meet the homeward-bound steamer about mid-ocean and exchange mails, and accordingly we waited day after day with our package of letters. When we had given up the steamer, we watched for whales, and some of these sea-monsters made their appearance near the ship; and then we took to watching the flying-fish as they came out of their native element, on short excursions in the upper air, with their silver bodies and transparent wings; they are as beautiful as birds, and their flight is by no means ungraceful; some of them flew from one to two hundred feet before going below to moisten their wings. The sea-birds never left us, even when more than a thousand miles from land, and I could not help feeling a deep sympathy for them living so far from the rest of the world, but if they prefer such a life I have nothing to say against it; I know they did not ask for any sympathy or seem to need it. They are very pretty birds, but some have given up the chase. Half a dozen sharks tried their swimming powers against the Colorado, but we beat them. For three days we made just the same gentle speed of two hundred and six miles a day; all is tranquil and serene, and in five times twenty-four hours we have one thousand and thirty miles out of the five thousand three hundred on a southern line to Yokohama. Our monotony has been twice broken by cries of fire, but these cries have only been uttered to call up officers and crew for exercise, and it is quite amusing to see the Chinese boys rush out from hatchways and every available porthole, and take up hatchets and buckets and apply the hose fore, aft, and amidship. On our voyage we passed through one experience, which was novel to most of us, and which occurs only on the Pacific Ocean. It was the dropping of a day out of the calendar; we retired to our state-rooms and fell asleep on Friday night, the 13th of November, 1874, leaving everything correct according to the almanac; when we awoke the next morning we found that it was Sunday, the 15th of November, and we had not overslept ourselves. I went to the room of the first officer, whose duty it was to keep the log of the ship, in which everything important is entered, and found he made the following record: "Sunday, November 15, 1874. Note.—Having crossed the prime meridian 180°, bound westward, Saturday, the 14th of November, is discarded, being called by name and date the next following as above." We were not without warning on the subject; indeed, it had been a matter of speculation for several days as we approached the 180° of longitude, west and east of Greenwich, and all the more interest attached to it from the uncertainty as to what day we should cross that meridian; had it been one day later a Sunday would have been blotted out, and we should have gone to bed on Saturday and got up on Monday; as it was we were called to adjust our feelings to what seemed an arbitrary change of the holy Sabbath from its proper place to one day earlier in the calendar; we did so, and kept the day as the Sabbath with clear consciences. Occasionally during the morning the thought would come into our minds that those we had left behind us were in the midst of Saturday, and that during our sleep we had made an extraordinary leap to get into Sunday; but so far as my own feelings were concerned, the Sabbath was as holy as any I have spent on sea or land after passing the one hundred and eightieth meridian degree of longitude east or west.

If there is any answer to the old problem, Where does the day begin? it is this: At the one hundred and eightieth degree of longitude east or west. This is the only line on which there is any arbitrary change or commencement of a day; but, as a practical thing, the day begins all round the world not at the same moment of time, but just as the sun visits different parts of the earth at successive periods in twenty-four hours. The time will never come when the day will begin all over the world at the same moment, or when the whole world will be keeping the same hours as the holy Sabbath, until the earth becomes a plane, instead of a globe. With the present shape of our world, it would be as much an impossibility as for the sun to rise upon every part of the globe at the same instant of time. If one of the members of the Seventh-day Baptist Church would accompany us around the world, having passed the prime meridian, we should both be keeping the same Sabbath, for he, of course, would be opposed to making any change. He would then be in harmony with the mass of Christians, as we pass along westward, but when we reached the United States, he would be one day in advance of the Church to which he belongs. He would then be a regular First-day Baptist.

EXCURSIONS IN JAPAN.

I have been at sea when the sight of land was

far more welcome; but it was a joy again to see the solid earth, and the green shores of Japan are among the most beautiful of any that skirt the seas. When the time arrived, and we drew near the shores covered profusely with verdure and foliage, the hills and the valleys had all the brilliancy of color of the Irish coast, with an endless variety of contour and an originality of surface that made the whole scene one of great beauty, without the element of grandeur. The sacred mountain of fire Fusiyama, the glory of Japan, which the Japanese, as by sense of religious duty, put into every picture and on every article that they manufacture, rose up about sixty miles distant. The volcano, though not active, forms a lively feature in the landscape. In clear weather it may be seen more than one hundred miles out at sea. As we steamed up the Gulf of Yeddo, the scene became more and more animated and Japanese in its aspect. Great numbers of fishing-boats, with their square sails rudely hung against the masts, were putting out from shore on their daily errand, and shoals of smaller boats, sculled by native Japanese, were plying around. Occasionally a palm-tree would show itself, but the pine and the fir and other evergreens, for which Japan is celebrated, abounded all along the shore. Now and then a bamboo grove, with its light bluish-green and feathery foliage, not one of the most beautiful, but really the most vegetable growth in the world, would diversify the velvety landscape. The narrow valleys running back from the water are green with rice-fields and the terraced hills with different crops.

YOKOHAMA.

We were soon entering the harbor of Yokohama, the principal port of Japan, in which vessels of all nations, men-of-war and merchantmen, were lying at anchor and giving the harbor a familiar look. The stars and stripes were displayed from a number of ships. The firing of our gun and the dropping of the anchor brought around us a swarm of native boats, all propelled with sculls by Japanese men and women almost as innocent of clothing as when they were born. In the course of the day our baggage was piled into one of the boats, and ourselves into another propelled by five lusty natives, who at every stroke of their sculls sent forth a groan or wail which would now and then break into a scream more novel than pleasing. We landed in the midst of a crowd of coolies nearly naked, and then came the strife for the baggage; but it was a far better-mannered crowd than one will find in any civilized country in which I ever landed. After the formality of opening one of our numerous trunks by a Japanese custom-house official, who politely bowed that it was all right, and did not wait for any fee, the crowd of nearly naked coolies divided off into separate squads, all remaining quiet while two or three of their number were making some arrangement, I could not tell what, in regard to our baggage. I soon found that they were preparing to draw lots to see which squad should have the porterage; the "lots" were little ropes of straws curiously intertwined and bound together by a band of straw; the band was severed, and with a shout the coolies all lifted their hands; four of the strands were found to be tied by another band indicating the four fortunate coolies; the rest submitted without a sign of dissatisfaction. The part of Yokohama which we entered on landing is not a Japanese town, but was built and is occupied by foreigners, and has none of the characteristics of a native city. There is no wharf,—a wide band or street extending nearly a mile along the water, on the shore side of which the foreign merchants have their bungalows and offices; some of these are surrounded with walls, the yards being ornamented with Oriental shrubbery and plants, including the beautiful evergreen. Many of the foreign merchants reside on the high bluff overlooking the town and bay, which affords a fine view of the country as it stretches out towards Fusiyama.

We remained in Yokohama over one steamer, in order to visit Yeddo by railroad and to make some excursions into the country. One of the most interesting objects is the statue of Daiboots, fifteen or twenty miles distant, and near the ancient capital of the Tycoons, the extinct city of Kanagawa. The whole region of country is strikingly beautiful, as is indeed the whole island, and so far as I have seen it the whole empire of Japan. Kanagawa is the residence of one of the daimios, a place of some importance and a charming spot. As we expressed a desire to dine, one of the Japanese went with a net to a tank near by, and in a few moments some of the excellent fish with which the waters of Japan abound were upon the coals, and it was but a short time until they were before us. Another was busied in preparing the universal beverage, which in Japan, as in China, is a simple infusion of tea without either milk or sugar, and almost without taste. There is no vegetable production in the East—none in the world—that is applied to more uses than the bamboo; not even the palm in all its varieties is more useful. The roots of bamboo are made into preserves, and the young shoots are eaten. The Japanese often built their houses of bamboo, beams, posts, rafters, siding, and thatch, while the scaffolding, ropes, and ladders are made of the same. Nearly every article of furniture in the house is bamboo: chairs, bedsteads and beds, stools, tables, and stands. Their most common utensils are made wholly or partly of bamboo: tools, brooms, buckets, dippers, and measures and boxes of all kinds, the chop-sticks with which they eat, baskets and trays. Ornaments of all kinds, musical instruments, umbrellas, cloth, paper, books, and pens come from the same source. Boats are built and rigged throughout of bamboo; scarcely anything in the whole economy of Japanese life can be named that is not made in whole or in part from this invaluable production of nature. In China, too, it is an important element in government, occupying a more indispensable place than birch in America. It is said that China could not be governed without the bamboo. A catalogue of its various uses would fill many pages. And now we are entering the suburbs of Yeddo, and now the city itself; the crowd increases and becomes more and more curious, the people all along the street, as if out on a holiday, stand and stare and laugh as we pass, as if we were the first of our kind ever seen in Yeddo.

YEDDO.

On reaching Yeddo we were driven to the Niphon Hotel, the finest hotel in the empire, and one that would not discredit any city in the world. Yeddo has one million eight hundred thousand inhabitants. The second morning we drove to a high bluff in the centre of the city, called Atangoreama, which is reached by a flight of stone steps, about a hundred in all. We were attended this time by nine Yakonin soldiers, who surrounded our carriages when we rode, and dismounted to accompany and protect us whenever we had occasion to walk. The heights of Atangoreama afford the finest view of the city, and overlook the castle or palace of the Tycoon, which, since the Tycoonate was abolished, is used for the purposes of the new government. The castle stands upon high ground, and is strongly fortified after the Japanese fashion, with walled terraces and deep, wide moats, making it almost impregnable to native attacks, although comparatively weak to those skilled in the more modern arts of war. A drive along the castles, walls, and moats is one of the great attractions of Yeddo. The city, which stretches out for miles in every direction, abounds in beautiful spots and interesting scenes, in which Japanese art has combined with nature to produce the finest effects.

ANCIENT CEMETERY.

These sacred grounds must have been laid out many centuries ago, and successive rulers have spent immense sums in adorning them and keeping them in order in Yeddo and Thiba. It covers a vast extent of ground, a hundred, perhaps hundreds of acres; we could not tell how many, for there was nothing to bound the vision when we were once within the inclosure. Entering by a massive gateway, we drove a long distance on a broad avenue shaded by magnificent old trees; we came at length to another arched gateway, where we left our carriages and passed into a square court of some acres, in which stands a temple exceeding in grandeur and splendor all that we had imagined of Japanese architecture. The exterior is heavily ornamented with carving, and the interior literally shone with burnished gold.

Leaving this temple, we passed to another part of the cemetery, and were conducted through a succession of courts and temples not so large as the first, but far more elaborately and beautifully ornamented. I was surprised by the refined taste shown in the combinations of colors and in the ornaments with which they were loaded.

Some of the wide court-yards inclosing temples were surrounded with porticoes or loggia, the roofs of which were exquisitely frescoed, with a beauty and modesty of coloring that I have never seen surpassed in any country; the paneling contained birds in endless variety painted as if from life. From Thiba we returned to Yokohama.

The Japanese are a reading people. I often found the servants when not on duty engaged in reading, and on one occasion I took the book from the hand of one of them and found it a profusely illustrated volume. Their reading is chiefly sensational novels, arranged with a pair of lovers, after the most approved style of French or English fiction.

JAPAN AND THE JAPANESE.

The territory of Japan contains four large islands and nearly four hundred smaller. There are seven grand divisions, which are subdivided into sixty-eight provinces, and these again into smaller districts and towns. It has an area of one hundred and ninety thousand square miles, and a population of twenty million. For the last six hundred years there have been both a civil and religious ruler, although the latter was scarcely anything more than a nominal officer. The former, known under the name of Taikun, or Tycoon, had the reins of government in his own hands, but the Mikado was recognized as the religious head of the country, and indeed was superior in rank to the Tycoon, although he had but little to do with public affairs, and his existence was regarded almost as a myth. In the year 1868 a revolution was inaugurated, and at length became successful, by which the power of the Tycoon was overthrown. He was reduced to the position of prince of the empire. The Mikado was duly installed as supreme ruler, and is now recognized as such throughout the empire. Below him are two hundred and sixty daimios, of whom eighteen are the great chiefs of the empire,—feudal lords, with supreme authority in their own provinces and having thousands of retainers; the two-sworded men of the country, a class of men who live upon the daimios, are supposed to do their fighting for them, and who are sometimes quite as ready to fight for themselves.

The Japanese, although far more agreeable in their manners than the Chinese, are both intellectually and physically inferior; they are quicker in apprehension perhaps, more imitative, and more willing to learn from others; they possess, or at least exhibit, more curiosity; they are decidedly very ingenious in manufacturing all kinds of goods, everything being made in first-rate order; but are wanting in mental vigor, as compared with others, neither do they have that overweening sense of their importance in the scale of being and of superior knowledge which belongs to the Chinese. Their bearing towards each other and towards the outside is regulated accordingly. In their houses and shops and in many of their industrial and domestic arrangements they are patterns of neatness and good taste. One may walk for miles through their streets, looking into their dwellings or places of business, which are all open by day, and he will never tire in his admiration of the cleanliness which prevails, and of the regard to order and general effect in the arrangement of their various wares and varying colors. One of the customs of married life is absolutely hideous. The Japanese generally have fine teeth; but when a woman marries, she is compelled by the laws of society to dye her teeth black, and this process is renewed every three or four days. In city or country, wherever you meet the grim smiles of the women who have fallen into the bonds of matrimony, they look more like hybrid monsters, with their black teeth, than like the lovely beings they ought to be. What was the origin of this custom I do not know; but there are only two things which have led me to desire temporary imperial authority in Japan: one is to establish some sort of costume for the men, and the other to abolish the custom of married women dyeing their teeth.

The beggars in Japan, as in many other countries, form a distinct profession, though not so numerous nor so imperious in their demands as in Europe, and in their moderation and apparent honesty are a model for the beggars of all nations. Seeing some forty or fifty coppers hanging on as many nails at the door of a shop (the copper coin has a hole in the centre), I inquired what they were for, and was told they were placed there by the shopkeeper to save time and trouble in answering the calls of the mendicants. When one came along, he simply took a copper and passed on, never abusing the charity of the shopkeeper by taking two. The device by which their calls are attended to might be worth imitation in other parts, if equally honest beggars could be found.

CRIMES.

Capital crimes are punished either by decapitation with the sword or by crucifixion ; many executions by the former mode have taken place in Japan; the latter has been common, and is still practiced. Each city has its execution-ground, which is often upon the high road; we passed those of Yokohama and Yeddo in going through the cities.

DISPOSAL OF THE DEAD.

Their mode of disposing of the dead is both by burial and burning, the wishes of the dying being considered by the friends imperative as to the mode in which the body shall be disposed of. In some parts of Japan burning is always practiced. A large furnace is connected with the cemetery, in which the body is speedily consumed, the ashes being carefully preserved and buried with as much solemnity as are the entire remains in other countries. Some of the cemeteries are very beautiful, covering a large extent of the hill-sides. The large cemetery at Nagasaki, as seen from the harbor, presents a very striking appearance,—tiers of tombs rising one above another in graceful terraces.

RELIGION.

The Japanese are not what we should call a religious people. The two prevailing forms of religion are Sintoism and Buddhism; but neither of these have a strong hold upon the people, or awaken deep religious feeling. Nowhere have I seen the manifestations of reverence, or anything approaching profound worship : even their temples are far from being accounted sacred; they are often made places of entertainment and continued residences for strangers; the first Protestant missionaries on coming to Japan had a temple assigned them as their home, and occupied it for a long period. When we entered the temple at Yeddo we were invariably followed by a curious crowd, but no one made a sign of prostration or engaged in any act of worship, or exhibited any respect for the place more than for ordinary buildings. Sintoism was the ancient faith of the country,—its hierarchy consists of the Mikado, two ecclesiastical judges, and the priesthood, which comprises also the monks.

The temples are usually on elevated places, or surrounded with trees; they have no idols in the temples. On the altar stands a mirror, which is regarded as an emblem of the purity required in the worshipers, and as requiring sincerity of worship. The form of worship is simple, first washing in the sacred font, the praying before the mirror to the great sun-goddess, making an offering of money or rice or its equivalent, and lastly, striking the bell to signify to the goddess that the worship is over. The bells connected with the temples are large, and are usually hung near the ground, where they can be easily struck.

Everything connected with Japan, and especially with the government, partakes more or less of mystery, and nothing more than the attitude of the government toward Christianity, edicts being issued and posted all over the country forbidding the people to embrace it, and at the same time calling into its service for the education of the youth Christian missionaries, who have come to the country with the avowed object of laboring for the conversion of the Japanese to Christ, leaving them wholly untrammeled as to what they shall teach. But with all that is mysterious or unfavorable, there is much to encourage hope in regard to the future of the country. The growing disposition to conform the administration of the government to the American model, and to introduce American science and arts, the increasing intercourse, official and social, with the United States, the sending of so many youth to be educated in the United States under the influence of our Christian institutions, and the calling into public service at home of so many Protestant Christian teachers, are remarkable signs which may well inspire hope.

THE TONSURE.

In Japan men shave their heads just where the Chinese do not, making a bald spot upon the crown, which likens them to Jesuit priests, while they leave a broad circle of hair around the head. Men and women shave the eyebrows off smooth, and have the hair carefully plucked out of the ears and nose. The barber is an important functionary in this part of the world, every person of high or low degree calling his services into requisition almost daily. Economically it might be regarded as a great expense to the nation, but on the other hand it affords employment and support for a large class.

JAPANESE HABITS.

Many of their habits are the exact opposites of those of other nations. The carpenter in using the plane always draws it towards him instead of pushing it; it is the same with the saw, which he draws when he wishes to cut, the teeth being set accordingly. One of their customs struck me as an improvement upon the mode of doing things in civilized countries, especially after I had acquired some knowledge of their vicious ponies. In stabling their horses they tie them with their heads to the door or front of the stable, so that they can approach them in front instead of behind, thus reducing to every-day practice the trick of the showman, who made a handsome sum by admitting visitors to see a horse whose head was where his tail ought to be. The horses, by the way, are generally shod with straw instead of iron. A straw mat is fastened upon the foot with cords of the same material, and so slightly that the streets in which horses are used are strewn with the cast-off sandals of the ponies.

INLAND SEA.

Inland Sea, December 5, 1874.—The most beautiful sea in the world is the Inland Sea of Japan, between three of the four largest islands, Niphon, Kioo-Sioo, and Sikoke. There is an expanse of water five hundred miles in extent from east to west, and varying greatly in breadth, connected at different points with the ocean, but forming a great land-locked sea. The name, like most Japanese names, is singularly beautiful, Suwonda. Into this wide expanse have been sprinkled more than three thousand islands, which by volcanic action have been moulded into all the forms of beauty imaginable. Some of them are lofty cones, rising directly from the water to the height of several hundred feet; others are rounded off with more variety of outline, and stretch away for miles with constantly changing profile, and with shores and hill-sides and valleys as green as emeralds. I have found nothing to compare with it in any other sea, and this is the testimony of every traveler I have met who has made the passage. We were two days and one night—a bright, beautiful moonlight night—in steaming through the sea, and, as I recall the voyage, the scene rises up before me like the vision of some fairy-land. During the whole passage the water had scarcely a ripple upon its surface, and an ever-changing panorama of green islands, of narrowing straits, expanding bays, picturesque landscapes, hills, and valleys, with cities scattered along the shore, rolled by us with constantly-varying beauty.

Early the next morning we anchored in the harbor of Hiogo, one of the open ports, and the most beautifully situated town in Japan. Osake, of which Hiogo is in reality the port, is fifteen miles distant, and is the site of the fortified castle of the Tycoons, destroyed by fire when the Tycoon left it in the late revolution. Osake, manufacturing a great quantity of the various kinds of silk, is a city of great wealth, its silk-houses surpassing those of any other city in the empire. Bamboo and plantain groves surround it. Hiogo gives promise of becoming an important place in the commerce of Japan; it certainly has great attractions as a residence. Hiogo has thirty thousand and Osake one million eight hundred thousand inhabitants.

We rose next morning at six, in time to see the gates of the East opened. Islands, with charming little bays, were around us. The country was under more perfect cultivation than any portion of the coast that I have seen, the terraces running far up the hill-side, and trees and shrubbery indicating the tastes of the inhabitants. On either side of the strait was a large city well fortified. Just at dark we came upon the Arched Rock, a small island jutting out from the sea, united at the top, but with a wide arch, some thirty or forty feet in height, under which boats can sail with ease. As the last rays of daylight were vanishing we entered the harbor of Nagasaki, on the extreme west end of Japan, which is completely concealed from the sea, running back around high headlands. Nagasaki has twenty thousand inhabitants.

NAGASAKI.

Our ship lay for one day and two nights in the harbor of Nagasaki, affording us an opportunity to visit the town and to enjoy the beautiful scenery, which, were it not on such a limited scale, would rival the grandeur of Hiogo. About midnight, the last night of our stay, I heard a whistling in the rigging of our ship, which assured me that the calm we had enjoyed so many days presaged a storm, and I was not disappointed.

THE STORM.

We prepared ourselves as best we could to withstand the blast, but we could not long keep the deck, and were forced to go below. All day long one crash after another was heard as a table broke loose or the steward's crockery went into a heap. Though in a staunch and mighty ship, we felt, what we had not occasion to feel before, how weak are the proudest works of man in contending with the breath of the Almighty! We could only commit ourselves to his care during the long, dark night, while the tempest raged and the great waves tossed us up and down. With the morning came a change: early in the day we entered the broad mouth of Yang-ste-kiang River, and quietly steamed toward Shanghai, thankful that we had reached another continent in safety, and that for a little while our tossings upon the deep were over.

A more perfect contrast than our experience upon the inland sea of Japan, and that upon the eastern China sea, could not well be imagined.

SHANGHAI.

We entered the Yanste River, as the Amazon is called, far out at sea. Long before we came in sight of the low shores, the water became as yellow as that of the Tiber, taking its color from the soil of the country, which is constantly washing down the river, filling up the wide mouth and making the navigation more and more difficult. We soon entered the Woosung, a small river on which Shanghai is situated, about twelve miles from its mouth. At the entrance is a long range of earthworks,—one of the supposed impregnable forts which the Chinese in their self-sufficiency and contempt of foreigners erected at various points, and which have proved equally efficient with the paper fortifications recommended in Salmagundi. They were easily battered to pieces by the English fleet in the war of 1841. Shanghai is one of the four ports first opened by the treaty of 1842. The climate is very trying in winter. The malaria of the low country was formerly productive of fevers, but, at a great expense, a system of draining and of street construction was carried out by which the health of the place has been improved. The cost of these improvements was so great that the Chinese say Shanghai is paved with dollars. The first thing that arrests a traveler's attention on landing is the novel mode of conveyance peculiar to Shanghai. The popular carriage is a wheelbarrow. The streets of the old city are narrow and rough, and so much broken up by bridges that this vehicle cannot be used; but in the foreign settlement you find the Chinese men and women everywhere on wheelbarrows. The wheel is much larger than those in use in our country, and the passengers are seated one on each side of it when two are riding; if they are of equal weight the carriage is evenly balanced, but when two persons of unequal weight are carried, or only one, the wheel is turned up at an angle, so that the weight shall come upon the point in its circumference that strikes the ground.

The Chinese part of the town has a population of nearly a million souls, including that portion built around the walls for want of room within. During the rebellion the number was almost twice as great. The city proper is entered by several gates, which are narrow passages admitting only what goes on foot. Everything in the shape of merchandise, and every stone and timber for building, is carried in on the shoulders of coolies, as in most parts of the East.

One will not be inclined to linger long in his walks through the native city, although he may see much at every step that is both novel and interesting. The Chinese shops, the Chinese costumes, sights, and smells of all kinds, are perfectly new, and, as he has never met them before, he will never wish to meet the most of them again. At several points as I was passing along I came upon police stations where criminals of different grades were undergoing different degrees of punishment. Some were simply confined in large cages,—the sport of the passers-by,—others wore immense collars made of two wide boards brought together at their edges, with a hole large enough for the neck; the collar is so wide that the prisoner cannot reach his head with his hands, and is dependent upon his friends or upon charity, not only for his food, but for getting it to his mouth; others had their heads jutting out of the tops of cages, which were so high that they could not sit down, and so low that they could not stand up, or in which they stood on tiptoe: they were condemned to pass days and nights in this uncomfortable and even torturing position. A short time before, several persons who were guilty of a capital offense were condemned to death and placed in these cages, where they died from starvation before the eyes of the people, no one being allowed to furnish them with food. Torture, as I subsequently learned by witnessing it at Canton, enters largely into the idea of punishment among the Chinese, and is freely resorted to for the purpose of extorting confession from the accused.

I expected to visit Pekin and the Great Wall of China, but was told it was too late in the season. We regretted not being able to visit the capital of the Flowery Kingdom; but it is as well to see a few Chinese cities. With the exception of Pekin, they are built pretty much after the same uninteresting model, the chief difference consisting of the degrees of filth. There is less of the beautiful in scenery in the country at large than in almost any country I have visited.

HONG KONG.

We reached Hong Kong at the end of the third day. Hong Kong is an island about twenty-five miles in circumference,—an English possession taken as an indemnity in one of the wars, and ceded to Great Britain in 1841. There is scarcely a level acre upon the whole island. The typhoon destroyed a great part of the city and shipping in 1874. I visited the Colonial Prison, where more than four hundred criminals of all nations were confined, and have never seen a penitentiary more neatly kept or apparently under better management. Among the prisoners were several Chinese women who had been convicted of child-stealing,— a very common crime. The boys are stolen and sold for boatmen, and the girls either for boat-hands, or for the brothels, to be educated for a life of infamy.

I inquired of the superintendent if any form of oath was administered to the Chinese when they were called upon to testify in the courts, and was informed that none was used in cases of small importance, but in graver cases they were sworn by a cock's head : the cock is taken to the Joss-house or temple, the head cut off with some ceremony, and on this, as basis of the most solemn oath that is administered, a Chinaman gives his testimony in an English court.

CANTON AND ITS SIGHTS.

Canton is situated on the Pearl River, ninety miles from Hong Kong, which is now the port of Canton, for scarcely a vessel goes up the river.

The business of the place and the foreign commerce is nearly all transacted at Hong Kong. An American river steamer leaves the latter port every morning at eight o'clock, and another returns each day at the same hour. The banks of the Pearl River are flat, but they are in a high state of cultivation, covered with rice-fields and plantations of bananas, which were looking green and fresh, and added much to the beauty of the shores. Twelve miles below Canton we reached Whampoa, once a place of some commercial importance, and soon after came upon the outskirts of the wilderness of boats, which forms one of the most remarkable sights of the great city. It is estimated that three hundred thousand of the people belonging to Canton live on the water in boats, not merely to obtain a livelihood from the water, but chiefly for the sake of a residence. The people are born, spend their days, and die in their boats,—the only homes and the only shelter they have from the time of their birth until they are committed to the grave; and yet a happier-looking class of people I have not seen anywhere in China. I saw father, mother, and eight little children taking their breakfast of rice and fish and a few greens in one end of the boat, apparently as well contented as if they owned a palace. These boats are of all sizes and all sorts, the most of them small sampans, about the size of an ordinary row-boat, with a simple mat or bamboo covering over one half, while others are large and elaborately ornamented with carvings in wood and gold and paint, and some of them are occupied as restaurants and places of amusement, the large boats being usually moored alongside of each other, with long water-streets running between the blocks; besides, there are innumerable crafts, junks of all sizes sailing or rowing up and down and across the river, making it exceedingly difficult at times to find an opening through which to steer a boat.

The men who live on the water go ashore for employment during the day, and the women ply the oars, and capital boat-hands they are. I gave them a decided preference over the men, for they are not only equally handy with the oar or the scull, but they are far more polite, and I may add more honest, than their other halves who are on shore at work during the day.

One would imagine that a boat must be a dangerous place to bring up a family of children; but the mothers tie a joint of bamboo to each of the little ones, and if they tumble overboard it serves as a float, and they are recovered. They do not grieve much if the child never turns up, especially if it be a girl.

TYPHOONS.

There have been some fearful scenes among the floating population. The typhoons which sweep over the China seas and along the coast, and which are so destructive to shipping, seldom come so far inland as Canton; but nine years since one of the most severe ever known passed over the city, and it is comparatively easy to imagine the havoc made with these floating homes of the poorer people, but impossible to describe or even conceive the scenes which followed. This wilderness of river-craft, which at ordinary times is so quiet and only swaying hither and thither with the tide, was like a heap of chaff before the tempest. The houseboats, many of which were of large size, became as dust to the wind, and were carried away no one knew where; the heavier boats were sunk in great numbers, the occupants were hurled into the water as their homes were torn to pieces, and when the storm had passed and an estimate could be made of the loss of life, it was found that sixty thousand persons had perished. For a long time the river was strewn with dead bodies.

Canton is regarded as the first city in the empire for wealth and elegance. It is the best built, and, what is no mean praise for a Chinese city, it is the cleanest. There is no external magnificence in any of the buildings; indeed, when a stranger enters the gates of this or any other city that I have seen in China he bids adieu to the outside world, and even to the heavens, and wanders on in a labyrinth until he leaves the city itself.

SILK-WEAVING.

The silk-weaving which is largely carried on at Canton is accounted among its curiosities, but is chiefly interesting as showing how the most beautiful fabrics can be wrought in small and dirty hovels, and with purity. All the silks of China, for which Canton is most celebrated, are woven by hand on the rudest of looms by mere girls and boys. I watched, with no little surprise, the growth of a fine brocade, a little boy managing the harness and a little girl sitting at the loom and casting the shuttle. Every figure came out of their hands perfect, the whole piece looking as if it had just come from the fuller without spot. The Chinese, too, are the reverse of neat in their personal habits, and one soon comes to associate this with the blue cotton clothing which is seen whenever clothing is used at all.

CHINESE MANNERS AND CUSTOMS.

Birds'-nests are a luxury in China, being within the reach of the wealthy alone; they are sold at prices graduated according to the quality of the article, none of any value bringing less than their weight in silver, and some bringing almost their weight in gold. Nests are sold as high as thirty or forty dollars per pound. Some naturalists maintain that the gelatin is formed from a sort of sea-foam, which the swallow gathers, and which is exuded from the mouth of the bird. It resembles the gelatin known by the name of isinglass, and the purer sort is almost transparent. The nests come chiefly from the island of Java, where they are obtained with great labor and often at much peril from deep caves along the coast. Some of these caves on the southern coasts are approached only by a perpendicular descent of great depth by means of ladders, the raging of the sea below preventing all approach from the water. When collected they are assorted into different grades, those which have not been occupied by the birds bringing the highest price, and other grades prices according to cleanliness and quality. From one to two million dollars' worth are imported every year into Canton.

ANIMAL FOOD.

The Chinese do not have as great a variety of animal food as the western nations, but they make use of some which most nations reject. In regard to the use of rats and puppies, I find a great diversity in the testimony of travelers and residents, some of the latter stoutly affirming that such animals are not eaten at all, or if so only in cases of extremity where nothing else in the shape of food can be obtained. But I have seen all these exposed for sale in the markets of Canton in the very heart of the city. There are several dog-markets where nothing else is sold, and where I have seen dogs dressed and ready-cooked. Rats also, alive and dead, fresh and dried, are regularly and constantly sold, and I have seen them in all these states of preparation as I have been passing by. One plump fellow I saw suspended by his tail from the market hook, waiting for a purchaser, but all the while struggling to escape, while the dried specimens hanging around him mocked his agony and awaited their destiny with more composure. There is no more reason for denying that such animals are regularly sold for food in the markets of Canton than that beef or mutton are sold in New York or Philadelphia.

SMALL FEET.

The cultivation of small feet is not altogether peculiar to the higher classes, nor to those who are exempt from labor. In every city great numbers of women—perhaps a quarter or more of the female population—may be seen toddling about the streets on their pegs, looking very much as if their feet had been cut off and they were walking on the stumps. It is difficult for them to balance themselves in walking, and they frequently resort to a third peg or cane to keep themselves straight. The custom of closely bandaging the feet from infancy is not so injurious as might be supposed, but it greatly interferes with locomotion.

TEA.

Every one who visits China or reads about it is naturally curious to learn something about the great staple of the country, which has become the common beverage of the world. The tea-plant is a shrub which, left to itself, would grow to the height of twenty feet or more, but as cultivated for the production of tea it is cut down and kept down to four or five feet in height. It is raised chiefly in the central regions; the leaves are gathered several times during the season, the earliest tender leaves being accounted the best. The first crop is usually gathered in the third year from planting, and at the end of about seven years the plants are renewed or cut down to the ground, new shoots springing up from the roots. Plants treated in this way will live for twenty-five to thirty years and produce good crops.

CHINESE REVENGE.

In China, when a man gets angry with another and wishes to be revenged upon him, instead of killing the object of his hatred he kills himself. The principle on which he does it is the supposition that the man whom he hates will be answerable for his murder, and will be more heavily punished by evil spirits in this world and in the world to come than if his life had been taken. It is certainly, for society, a safer mode of administering vengeance than that which prevails in civilized countries, where the pistol and the bowie-knife are made to do their work upon unsuspecting victims.

PREPARING FOR DEATH.

The Chinese have a custom, quite peculiar to themselves, of ordering their coffins and having them sent home long before they have any thought of dying. They take peculiar pride in selecting the best materials, having them made good and strong, and, when they can afford it, in the most expensive style; and then they take great pleasure in showing them to their friends, keeping them where they can be seen by all who call.

RELIGIONS OF CHINA.

The prevailing forms of religion in China are Confucianism, Buddhism, and Tauism. The former, which is the faith of the educated and influential classes, is more a system of philosophy and of morals than a religion : it is founded on the teachings of the great Chinese sage, who flourished about five centuries before the Christian era, whose reputed writings contain a vast amount of practical wisdom and pure morality. Buddhism is an importation from India, where it had its rise, and from which it passed over Eastern Asia and to the adjacent islands. Tauism lays claim rather to the vulgar classes : it is a mystic sort of religion, deals in incantations and astrology, and, like spiritualism, pretends to intercourse with the departed dead as well as the acknowledged evil spirits. The priests are generally ignorant men, and through mystic art, and by playing upon the superstition of the people, maintain their ascendency over them.

GAMBLING.

The Chinese are all gamblers,—gambling everywhere, and for everything. Even the little boys, as I have often seen in going up to the fruit-stand, almost invariably cast the die to determine whether they shall have double or nothing for their money.

SHIPWRECKS.

The following account of the loss of the steamers

Japan and Hong Kong is taken from a newspaper published in Hong Kong:

"TOTAL LOSS OF THE JAPAN.

" With much regret do we announce the loss—and that one of the saddest nature—by fire—of the Pacific Mail Steamship Company's steamer Japan.

" We give such particulars as have reached us to the latest moment of going to press.

" Immediately upon receipt on Saturday of intelligence we issued extras which we subjoin:

" 9 A.M.

" Another misfortune has befallen the Pacific Mail Steamship Company in the total destruction by fire of the above excellent, valuable, and well-known craft. The intelligence reached Hong Kong at five o'clock this morning, when a boat arrived from the scene of the sad disaster.

" Our information is that at eleven thirty P.M., on Thursday the 17th, a fire was discovered in the hold when the Japan was about forty miles south of Swatou Light. We cannot gather that the mails or anything was saved.

" The Japan, Captain Warsaw, was a sister ship to the Alaska, of similar tonnage, built about seven years since. For two hours every possible effort was made to subdue the conflagration, but in vain, when the boats were necessarily resorted to.

" Five boats made, it is believed, for land, while a sixth sailed for this port, bringing the chief engineer, seven of the Chinese crew (including the cook's assistant), and a lady passenger.

"There were four hundred and twenty Chinese passengers, and, from the limited number of boats, it is naturally feared there must be a sad loss of life. A coast-steamer is hourly expected, when we may glean further information.

"The Yangtsze passed the *locale* of the loss, but did not perceive a vestige of the ill-fated Japan.

"2 P.M.—We gather that the crew were one hundred and twenty in number, so that in all there were some five hundred and forty souls on board. The catastrophe occurred one hundred and thirty miles from Hong Kong, near to Breakers Points. There were also twelve boats on board and a raft which could be made available for one hundred and fifty people, but we fear was not launched.

"We learn that the lady passenger, Mrs. Strott, who arrived in the first boat (at five A.M. this day), has been removed to Government House, and is being kindly and carefully attended by Miss Kennedy. This morning, at nine o'clock, a second boat arrived here, containing the stewardess, the baker and eight Chinese.

"From one of the survivors we gather that at about eleven thirty P.M., while asleep in his bunk, he was aroused by the butcher, and informed that a fire had broken out. He clothed himself scantily and proceeded on deck, and saw that the hose was being prepared and taken down to the engine-room, from which flames were proceeding. The captain was on the spot, and was superintending. The flames were very strong and the engines had been stopped, and the engineers and assistants had gone topside. The flames soon communicated to fore and aft and to the ladies' cabin.

"The chief mate some ten or fifteen minutes after advised every one to take care of themselves. For some time, however, water was continued to be thrown down, but in vain.

"With the purser and butcher our informant went to the mail-room to try and secure the mails, when flames threw out, bursting the bulk-head, and they were obliged to make a speedy exit. Returned on deck and went on the hurricane-deck, and seeing a boat being lowered, jumped in from the guard, on the starboard side; in this boat were the stewardess and eight Chinese.

"Were nearly three hours in getting away, the sea being very rough. At last succeeded in drifting away, at which time the fire was coming up through the engine-room and centre of the vessel, and the water was quite black with Chinese who had thrown themselves overboard.

"Succeeded in making sail the next morning, and about seven o'clock ran against a fishing-junk, and, striving for Swatou, arrived at two o'clock. The boat was taken on deck, and reached Hong

Kong at nine A.M., 19th. Two of the Japan's boats were chock full. The fire, it was thought, was over the boilers.

"There were two cabin passengers (gentlemen), one lady passenger, and two gentlemen in the steerage.

"The last seen of the captain was on the hurricane-deck, when he was going forward. There was not any land in sight.

"At noon on Thursday were about three hundred and nine miles from Hong Kong, and should have arrived at two o'clock on Friday. There was not time for any one saving even an article of clothing, except what they had on.

"The Saco and Yantic have left for the scene of the disaster.

"Of the seven boats which were lowered, none other than the two previously mentioned have as yet reached this port.

"Our evening contemporary has 'piled up the agony' pretty well in their extra issued on Saturday, but has evidently again been 'crammed' (like unto its report of the Florencio) in its details. We believe the Japan left on the 14th, not on the 11th; that it was due here at two P.M., and not eight A.M. on Friday; that considering the sad occurrence took place one hundred and thirty miles from Hong Kong, eight hours' steaming seems a good rate of speed; that there were five hundred and forty persons on board, not four hundred and fifty; that seven boats, not five, were lowered; that the calamity occurred one hundred and thirty miles, not eighty, from here.

"No reliable information could have arrived at by the 'Mail' as to nine-tenths of the crew being saved, but out of four hundred and twenty Chinese passengers only three saved is absurd, as by evidence we have procured. The statements as to the stewardess falling overboard into the boat just as it had been lowered, sustaining such injuries as to compel her to keep to her bed on arrival here; that the purser and doctor were seen floating about without signs of life; that the captain was seen standing on the deck enveloped in flames, are 'great crams.' Evidently the 'Mail' has been 'taken in,' as our American cousins would say.

"The chief engineer (Mr. Cosgrave) is located at the Pacific Mail Steamship's office. Mrs. Strott is under the kind care of Miss Kennedy; and the stewardess is with Mrs. Moore (Lammert, Atkinson & Company). The two European cabin passengers were a Mr. Gilbert, and Dr. Tyndal, a consul at Canton.

"It was believed there was considerable treasure on board the Japan, so that altogether the loss will be a serious one.

"Below we give the evidence of one of the Chinese crew. We incline to the hope that if either of the boats were capsized, most of the previous occupants were rescued.

"The Agamemnon, from Foochow, arrived yesterday morning at nine o'clock, but the captain had not heard even of the loss of the Mongol, and had not noticed en route anything of the remains of the Japan, of the loss of which he was not aware.

"The Chinaman states: 'I came from San Francisco, which we left on the 14th of November. We had some rough weather. On the 17th, at half-past eleven P.M., as a rigger, I was on watch, when I saw smoke coming up the hatches. A sailor rang the ship's bell, which gave the alarm. The Chinese sailors rushed up on deck. There were twelve boats besides the captain's gig. I got into one of the boats on the starboard side with the chief engineer and six Chinese sailors. Our boat was the sixth lowered; it was a large one. When I left, from the dense smoke, I could not see any one on deck. They must all have got into the other boats. I did not see any one swimming about in the water. Mrs. Strott was in another boat, which being too full we went alongside of, and I helped to pull the lady into the boat. She had not any boots or shoes on, and only one dress. I suppose we got away about one or half-past one A.M. All the other boats had left. I did not see the captain in any of the boats. Had he remained on board he could have got into our boat. The sea was very rough. We got away quick. As we left, the flames were coming up fore and aft, and from the engine-room. We had hard biscuits, as one hundred pounds are always put in each large boat, and two barrels of water (fifty pounds and one barrel of water being put in small boats). After about half an hour we succeeded in hoisting our sails and made for Hong Kong. We did not see any of the ship's boats. It was rough until we got to the Lye-ee-moon Pass. We did not ask assistance from the Chinese boats we passed, as ours was good enough. The lady was very sick, poorly and cold, and we wrapped a portion of our clothing around her. She did not, however, lie down. We reached Hong Kong and landed at the Canton wharf about five o'clock. We were all sick, more or less, and the engineer, having swallowed so much smoke, vomited nearly all night. At the breaking out of the fire smoke came up all along the deck. We took the lady to Boston Jack's; the engineer went to the office, and the Chinese found their way to their friends' houses. I do not know what caused the fire or where it broke out. For about an hour after the fire all the hose was used until the flames came up and drove those engaged away. Our boat was thought to be too heavy to be lowered, but we succeeded with much trouble, the engineer assisting.'

"*Sunday afternoon*, 3 P.M.—Since the above was in type the Yesso arrived between one and two P.M. this day, and on dispatching our shipping reporter, anxiously waiting his return, we had sincere gratification and thankfulness in immediately issuing as an extra the following official report from the captain of the Japan, and a report from the Yottung. It is impossible as yet to give a return as to the number of lives lost, all the boats not having been heard of, but we live in hopes that they may turn up and that more lives have been saved, including D. Tyndal (consul at Canton), Dr. Yates (surgeon), and others.

"The P. M. S. S. Co.'s steamer Japan, four thousand three hundred and fifty-one tons, E. R. Warsaw, commander, left San Francisco November 14, at noon, with twenty-four cabin, five European steerage, eight Japanese, and four hundred and twenty-two Chinese passengers, three hundred and seventy-five tons cargo, one hundred and sixty-eight boxes treasure, value three hundred and fifty-eight thousand five hundred and eight dollars, and twenty-one packages mail.

"Had pleasant weather, with variable winds, during passage to Yokohama, arriving there on December 10, 10.40 A.M., landed twenty-two cabin, four European steerage, eight Japanese, four hundred tons cargo, and sixteen packages mails. Received on board one European steerage, three Chinese passengers, forty-five tons cargo, six hundred tons coal, one bag mails, stores, etc.

"Sailed from Yokohama on the 11th, at four P.M., for this port; experienced pleasant weather up to noon of the 17th, when the wind freshened into a strong breeze from northeast with high sea; at nine P.M. passed Lammock Light, distant five miles, under sail and steam; at 11.25 P.M. Breaker Point, bearing west half south, distant twenty-six miles, strong northeast monsoon, with rough sea, when the fire was first discovered and the engines stopped. The ship headed in shore, ventilators turned from wind, all five engines working in perfect order, every effort made to subdue the fire; at same time officers detailed to secure all boats preparatory to saving life. Every effort to save the mails proved fruitless, and, finding it impossible to subdue the fire, we abandoned the ship with last boat at one A.M. December 18, the ship then being enveloped in flames amidships directly in engine and fire-rooms, all communication being cut off between forward and aft part of the steamer.

"Remained until noon in the vicinity of the wreck saving life, and engaged a fishing-junk to assist; cruised in the vicinity of the wreck, and succeeded in saving one hundred and seventeen souls from boats and water.

"Seeing no more prospect of saving life, stood in for Cup Chi point. At 6.30 P.M. intercepted the British steamer Yottung, Captain Koch, who kindly took us on board and conveyed us to Swatow, where we were transferred to steamer Yesso for Hong Kong.

"I beg to convey, on behalf of my officers, crew, and self, our sincere thanks to the English and American consuls at Swatow, Captain Koch and officers of the steamer Yottung, Captain Ashton and officers of the steamer Yesso, for their great kindness in rendering every possible assistance.

"Saved, one cabin passenger, Mr. Crocker, twenty-four European crew, sixty Chinese crew, thirty-four Chinese passengers.

"Missing, D. Tyndal (United States consul at Canton), Dr. Gates (ship surgeon), Mr. Bennett (first assistant engineer), two quartermasters, Harris and Sutton, Martin Cusack (cook), one steerage passenger.

"E. R. WARSAW,
"Late Commander of the S. S. Japan.

"The steamer Yottung arrived at Swatow on the 19th, having picked up the captain, officers, and ninety-four Chinese from the wreck of mail-steamer Japan. The Yesso left Swatow at 2.45 and proceeded to the place where it was supposed the wreck of the Japan was to be found. Searched for the wreck until midnight, but could not find her, the weather being hazy. On the 20th proceeded to Hong Kong."

"LOSS OF A PASSENGER STEAMER.

"The following telegram was received yesterday at Lloyds', dated Aden, February 26, eleven A.M.:

"The Hong Kong steamer, from London to Japan, struck on a sunken rock off Abdel Kuri, and foundered.

"Second mate and eighteen of the crew took to the boats, were picked up, and brought here by the Tiara steamer. Captain and seventeen of the crew left the vessel, and have not since been heard of. A lady and five children lost. The owners of the Hong Kong, Messrs. Watts, Milburn & Co., have also received from Messrs. James Burness & Son a telegram despatched yesterday at 8.36 A.M. from Messrs. Luke, Thomas & Co., of Aden, in the following words:

"'Inform owners immediately steamer Hong Kong struck sunken reef off Abdel Kuri islands and foundered. Lady passenger, five children, mate, chief and third steward, cook, fourth engineer, and butcher drowned; eighteen men arrived: captain, seventeen (second boat) missing.'

"The Hong Kong was an iron screw-steamer with four bulkheads. She was two hundred and ninety feet long, thirty-five feet broad, and twenty-five feet deep, and was built in 1871. Her gross tonnage was one thousand eight hundred and eighty-one; her burden two thousand eight hundred tons. She was classed A 1 at Lloyds' and fully insured; her value is estimated at about forty thousand pounds, and she carried, beside, a valuable cargo. The Hong Kong was a fast China liner, and had twice made passages with new season's tea, which were claimed as the fastest, though she did not start or arrive first. Her master was Captain W. G. Conley, who had, till he recently succeeded Captain Symmington, been chief officer of the same vessel. Both he and his officers were certificated. The Hong Kong left Gravesend on January 24, and arrived at Port Said on February 10. Here she was to disembark Mr. Webster, of the Port Said and Suez Coal Company, who was one of her passengers. She left Port Said on the 11th, passed Suez on the 13th, and must then have made her passage down the Red Sea and passed the Bab-el-Mandel Strait. The steamer was to touch first at Penang, afterwards at Singapore, then at Hong Kong, Yokohama, and Hiogo. The last point on the African coast she had to pass was Cape Guardafui, which is at the heel, as it were, of the African boot, and is at the northeastern extremity of Somaliland.

"Between the promontory and the island of Socotra, in latitude about 14° north, longitude about 53° east, lie a number of islands and rocks. It was here she struck, and it was not far from here that the same owners lost the Singapore in 1873.

"It is not difficult to identify the unfortunate family which has lost six members. In the list of passengers furnished to us by the owners occurs the name of Mrs. Jane Walton, with her children, Alfred, Esther, Jane, Thomas, and Nellie, and, according to the brokers, this lady was going out to join her husband at Yokohama. The other passengers were only three in number, namely, Mr. Colding, Mr. E. B. Peterson, and Mr. H. J. Lorne. The first mate, who is described in the telegram as drowned, was Mr. F. L. Murphy. The five others who made up the total of twelve people known to have perished were: E. Pittman, chief steward; W. Phelps, third steward; C. Stocking, the cook; W. Smith, fourth engineer, and the butcher. Including the captain, there were forty persons among the crew, and there were nine passengers after Mr. Webster left. The fuller telegram—that for the owners—tells us of twelve drowned, eighteen saved, and eighteen who escaped in a boat but were not picked up by the Tiara. This leaves one out of the forty-nine persons in the ship unaccounted for; but it is possible that one of the firemen was left at Suez, or, of course, that a slight inaccuracy was committed in the hurry of dispatching the news.

"The following is a list of the crew, exclusive of

those already mentioned by name. No one is described as butcher:

"A. Pakeman, second mate; F. Lawford, third mate; Henry Fisher, boatswain; David Nicoll, carpenter; James Tagg, lamp-trimmer; Jno. Orr, W. Robertson, E. Amos, and E. Borman, quartermasters; W. Wood, George Lord, Wm. Unwin, John Crawford, H. Champ, S. London, John Champion, and James Lang, able-bodied seamen; T. Wilkinson, chief engineer; F. O'Neill, second engineer; John Taylor, third engineer; T. Gillis, donkey-man; G. M. King, storekeeper; A. McKenzie, R. Hyder, G. Shenk, A. Von Tienen, J. Cornish, T. Burns, John Fernly, and George Minchin, firemen; E. Moorcraft, engineer's steward; E. Pettman, chief steward; G. Von Shultz, second steward; Ah Fat, second cook; Jose Da Costa, pantry-boy.

"The Hong Kong was laden with a general cargo of two thousand four hundred tons, which included three hundred tons of gunpowder for Japan. The Somalis, on whose coast the missing vessel is expected to be found, have been recently described by Sir Bartle Frere. He says 'they are a handsome, active, intelligent race, more akin to the Arab than the Negro, and little known and much distrusted in the last generation by our own naval officers. They are now distinguished in their employment at Aden as fishermen, laborers, and horse-keepers, etc., for their industry, intelligence, activity, and fidelity. Their occupations in their own country are generally pastoral.' It is added that they have recently taken to importing negro slaves at the rate of four thousand per annum, that they have always retained as slaves captives taken in war, and 'they seem to have been in the habit of keeping in their country any stranger who once entered it, and not allowing them to go away.' Probably since the British occupation of Aden this practice has been checked, but it is satisfactory to learn that a government vessel has gone in quest of the missing boat and the eighteen persons it contained.

"TELEGRAM FORWARDED FROM INDIA OFFICE.

"ADEN, February 26.

"'The Hong Kong struck on sunken rock of Abdel Kuri, near Socotra, five A.M. February 22, from Colombo to Liverpool (London for Japan), and foundered in eight minutes. Boat's crew of eighteen men arrived here, picked up by the Tiara steamer. Boat containing captain and seventeen men missing. Twelve persons drowned, among them lady passenger, Mrs. Daltern, and five children. Her Majesty's ship Kwantung sails immediately in search of missing boat, which may be found on Somali coast.'"

"ANOTHER WRECK.

"Intelligence has been received at Drogheda,

reporting the total wreck of an American bark of eight hundred tons' burden. A bucket and spars were washed ashore, bearing the name of 'Bell Hill.' She now lies within one hundred yards of the shore, on the rocks of Balbriggan. Three men have been washed ashore, completely exhausted, and two of them, although they received the best attention, have since died. The ship left Liverpool yesterday, bound, it is supposed, for Kingstown, and was caught in the storm."

FROM HONG KONG TO SINGAPORE.

After we had all—Jews and Gentiles, Persians, Hindoos, Mohammedans, and Americans—became acquainted, we had a very pleasant time during the voyage. Nor was religious conversation debarred. Oriental and Western politeness allowed us to speak freely of each other's views without any offense being given. It would be rare to find so many religions represented where such freedom of intercourse and conversation was enjoyed. We had but fairly got out of the harbor, and from under the shelter of the headlands, when we caught the monsoon blowing fresh and strong. It was a delightful sensation, after five days' incessant tossing, to feel once more at rest, and still more delightful were our sensations when we stepped ashore, and found ourselves in an earthly paradise, —the most enchanting spot that I have ever looked upon in any latitude or in any clime. As I wandered through the groves of spices and palm, and every form of tropical and oriental vegetation, I caught myself continually repeating the words of the old Mogul inscription, "If there be a paradise on earth, it is this, it is this."

SINGAPORE.

Singapore is situated on an island of the same name just at the extremity of the Malacca Peninsula. It is an English colony, having been ceded to Great Britain in 1824. Some one has explained the name as meaning the place of lions,—rather an extraordinary name for a place where lions were never known. The island once abounded with tigers, which are still occasionally met with. It is said that in former times they carried off and ate one man a day on an average. A resident of more than twenty years, who had made the languages of the East a study, informed me the word Singapore means a place to touch at. This is very appropriate, for it is in reality the touching place for all steamers which pass eastward or westward, from whatever quarter they come. Constant communication is kept up with the rest of the world, and scarcely a day passes without a visit from one or more of the grand fleet of steamers which are driving sails from the Eastern waters, as they have driven them from the Atlantic.

Singapore is not an undesirable place for a residence, being on the great high road of the nations east and west, but its chief attractions are its delightful climate and its rare productions. Situated only one degree north of the equator, it enjoys perpetual summer, and the atmosphere being moist from the vicinity of the sea and from the frequent showers with which it is visited at all seasons, the heat is never oppressive, the thermometer seldom rising above ninety degrees. I have before me the meterological record of an entire year, in which the highest temperature noted was eighty-eight degrees, and the lowest seventy-three degrees in winter.

NUTMEG GROVE.

At the invitation of the proprietor, we took a morning walk into a grove of nutmegs occupying several acres: the trees grow to the height of about twenty-nine or thirty feet, resembling pear-trees in general appearance, and bear fruit about the size and shape of a Sickel-pear: the grove was in full bearing. Every morning a man walks through, carefully examining each tree to see if the fruit has opened, the cracking of the outer shell being an indication that the nutmeg is fully ripe. This opening of the shell reveals an inner case of the brightest vermilion, the ordinary mace of commerce; and when this is removed the nutmeg is found in a third shell, much harder than the outside ones. I gathered several specimens, preserving some of them in their original trifold envelopes.

This plantation has on it twelve thousand cocoanut-trees, and fifteen hundred nutmeg-trees, with cinnamon, cloves, and all kinds of spices. The clove grows in large clusters upon the extremities of the branches of a large tree, and was in season when we were at Singapore.

PLANTATION.

The Rev. Mr. Keasburg, who has spent more than thirty years as a missionary at Singapore, and who, although not connected with any society, is still prosecuting his work vigorously,—preaching, teaching, and superintending a printing establishment that is sending out among the various classes of natives, and into other regions along the Malacca coast and among the islands, a knowledge of the gospel, has reclaimed from the jungle, about two miles out of town, a small plantation, which yields all the fruits and spices of the tropics with a profusion of shade made more delightful by its fragrance. Among the trees and shrubs that I saw in his grounds were the following: pineapple, cocoanut, bread-fruit, orange, mango, jack-fruit, mangostine, durian, custer-apple, coffee, chocolate, nutmeg, clove, cassia, etc., together with a variety of shade and ornamental trees, among which was the banyan.

THE FAN-PALM.

We took dinner with Mr. Keasburg on the 30th of December, 1874. The drive to his plantation was one of the most beautiful imaginable, the road being lined with bungalows and plantations laid out with exquisite taste, and adorned with all the luxuriance of tropical vegetation. One of the most conspicuous trees upon the island was the fan-palm,—not the palm from which fans are made, but a large tree having the symmetry and shape of a fan, as flat as if it had been placed in a press, although the circle of the leaves alone is at least twenty feet in diameter. It resembles the tail of a peacock when fully spread. This singular tree is also called the traveler's fountain, on account of the large amount of water secreted by it, which flows out when the tree is punctured, affording to the traveler an abundant supply.

One cannot go amiss at Singapore in looking for the beautiful: the whole island is covered with what seems a spontaneous growth of all that is graceful and attractive in vegetation, and animal life is not wanting to enliven the scene.

The jungle and forest abound in birds of the richest plumage; tribes of monkeys chatter among the branches of the trees, and occasionally a tiger makes his appearance when hard pressed for something to eat, and often devours a man.

MISSIONS.

Singapore was once a very important missionary station, not so much in its relation to the permanent population of the place, as on account of its affording an opportunity to exert an influence upon China and other neighboring countries. It was a standing place on which to operate while the Celestial Empire was closed against foreigners. For a long period there has been a large Chinese population on the island,—so large as really to afford a broad field for the missionary to work.

POPULATION.

Singapore, for its size, has the most conglomerate population of any city in the world, almost every nation being represented. The variety in costume and appearance strikes the stranger at once; it was the more noticeable to us coming from Japan and China, where the ordinary dress of the people is entirely uniform,—a dull-blue cotton. The wharf as we were leaving was one of the gayest scenes that we have met with. A large crowd, in all the colors of the rainbow, occupied the bank: there were Jews and Jewesses, elegantly dressed and glittering with jewels; Americans, the ladies fine-looking and splendidly dressed; Mohammedans, Bengalese, and Malays, in all sorts of bright colors, and many of them in plain dark color,—that in which they were born; then there were English and French and other Europeans in their own national costumes; besides the people, there was a grand display of gay-colored birds for sale,— parrots in green, crimson, yellow, white, etc. While we were waiting for the steamer to be off, boys, who seemed to belong to some amphibious tribe, amused the passengers by diving from boats for pieces of money thrown into the water, invariably catching them before they reached the bottom, which was about twenty-five feet below. In the midst of this variegated scene the order was given, and we were once more upon the sea.

PENANG.

Next is Penang. One Jew maintained that they might go ashore, but not go out in carriages, as that would be contrary to the command, "Seven days shalt thou labor," etc., this being the form in which he repeated it, and according to which he had probably been most accustomed to observe the day. Another thought it right to ride an elephant on the Sabbath, but not to ride in a carriage. The result of the discussion was that some went on shore and spent the day as they chose, while others, more conscientious, remained on board and played cards for money.

McDonald is the only missionary now at Penang, and his labors are distributed among the various races which compose the population of the town, among which, very strangely, the Chinese appear to be the most numerous. They occupy a separate portion of the city, forming a distinct community. The Celestials, indeed, are scattered through all the cities of East India.

ANIMAL LIFE.

These tropical regions are prolific of animal life as of vegetable. The most venomous snakes are quite at home in all these beautiful places, and they do not disdain an inviting bungalow for a residence. As we were driving through the city of Penang, a house was pointed out to me in which the proprietor found, on coming home one day, two boa-constrictors occupying his parlor, and waiting to give him a warm embrace; but he declined the compliment, and chose to have them put out of the way.

Left Penang at ten o'clock on the 2d of January, 1875, for the

BAY OF BENGAL.

The bay was like a mirror, and scarcely was a dying swell from a wave to be seen; the air was delightfully warm, and in the calmness which settled down over the sea great numbers of flying-fish, tempted from their native element to try their wings in a lighter atmosphere, skimmed along the surface in flocks; immense sea-turtles also came to the surface to sun themselves, and were not roused from their slumbers until we were just upon them. These waters are inhabited by snakes which sometimes reach a large size, very inconveniently making their way into cabin-windows, or on deck, when a stray rope hangs over the side by which they can work their way on board. We saw them, but happily had no visit from them on board. Some of our passengers took the precaution to close their ports, lest they should find in their cabins these unwelcome visitors.

We left the Straits of Malacca at three o'clock on the 2d of January, 1875, and started once more on the open sea for Point De Galle, or Ceylon. It took six days to go from Penang to De Galle. Put up at the Oriental Hotel; arrived January 7, 1875.

THE HARBOR OF GALLE.

Here the thermometer is eighty or ninety degrees in winter. It is very warm at present. We took a drive of seven miles, and visited the cinnamon groves and neighboring gardens, realizing more than the poetic sentiment of Ceylon's spicy breezes.

Galle's productions are the cinnamon gardens, cardamom, coffee, sugar, pepper, cocoanuts, coir cotton-cloth, jagery, fine cabinet-wood, shells, rice, grain, tobacco, bread-fruit, manganese, iron, silk, hemp, indigo, rubies, topazes, sapphires, amethysts, garnets, pearls, etc. From Galle to Colombo the country is rich in palm-trees; there are no less than twenty million majestic trees in the island, which has two million inhabitants, and Point De Galle has about thirty thousand inhabitants.

MISSIONARIES.

From many disparaging sentiments I had heard by the way about missionaries, their work and their converts, I was the more anxious to obtain information as to the facts of the case, and it was pleasant to hear from the Rev. Mr. Marks, missionary, that their lives and conduct would bear comparison with the average of home professors. He also informed me that the great want of Ceylon was more laborers to gather the ripening harvest of missionary culture. Galle itself is close, and the air is damp; but it is a most beautiful city.

MADRAS.

We left Point De Galle on the 17th of January for Madras, reaching that place in three days' sail. Stayed there one day. Madras has a population of about three hundred thousand; it is a fine city. We took a carriage and drove all through the place, visiting the Juggernauts and the monstrous car on which they are annually exalted; but the gods, the people, the cars, and the priests, all look like decay, and the annual turn-out is regarded more as a holiday than a religious ceremony. The gods are rivals, and each have their partisans. There have been thousands of people crushed by this wheel. The people of India come from all parts, lie down and let the wheels pass over them, crushing them instantly. This they think secures their going to heaven. The car on the wheels is about thirty feet high; the wheels, six in number, are six feet in diameter, and fourteen inches wide.

We went to see the botanical gardens in this city; we saw all kinds of monkeys, and wild animals; the garden was beautiful and splendid. We visited the place where they burned their dead; there were several then burning in the place, and as the guards stirred them up we could see the bodies. Their nearest relatives put up an urn made of clay, take the ashes, put them into the urn, which is made tight and thrown into the sea. They expect the souls to go to heaven.

We went all through Madras, which is a very difficult port to enter.

THE SURF

runs very high, sometimes making it impossible to land. We landed when the sea was calm, and it was even then difficult. Two men carried us from the sea to the shore, and the same way back again.

We left Madras at one o'clock on the 20th of January, 1875, and took the sea for Calcutta.

CEYLON.

We received a visit this morning from Signor Caprani, a young Italian, who speaks English with great fluency; he is one of the lieutenants of Thomas Cook, the great organizer of traveling tours, and is in charge of a small party of travelers who left London on the 4th of September, and have reached Ceylon after traversing the States of the great American Republic, exploring much of Japan, and seeing not a little of the Chinese Empire. Only five of the party are traveling through Ceylon, where they will remain till Saturday next, when they proceed to Calcutta. Kandy, Gampola, Nuwara Eliya, the Hakgala Gardens, Dimbula, and Nawalapitiya, are places on the list of the leader of the party to be visited in the next few days. They left for Kandy by the afternoon train to-day.

It may be not uninteresting to give a brief *résumé* of the places visited by these gentlemen since they left London, little more than three months ago. New York was the first place where they "rested the sole of their foot," and here they stayed for five days, proceeding thence to Philadelphia and Washington, which places were well "lion"ed. From the capital of the Republic they proceeded northwest through the oil region of Pennsylvania, where they "struck ile" in the shape of unsavory recollections of injustice done to the olfactory nerves; but soon after reaching Niagara, the feast of wonder provided by Nature for eye and ear relieved the other and offended organ. Chicago was the next halting-place, and here was surely sight-seeing in abundance: the great gaps where fire had so disastrously raged, the famous stores of the great grain city on the shore of Lake Michigan, and the State Exhibition then in "full swing." Two days were spent in Salt Lake City, the sacred city of Mormonism. An interview with that clever, worldly-wise man, though arch-impostor, Brigham Young, who was designated by one of the party as "a fine-looking old man, but a great scamp nevertheless," was obtained contrary to expectations, Brigham being in ill health. It seems that one of the apostles, Joseph Smith, had been a member of a Cook's tourist party through Palestine, and as soon as he heard that a detachment of that great army was in Utah and wished to see the "much-married" man, as Artemus Ward called Brigham, he used his influence to procure an interview, to the great gratification of Signor Caprani and his friends. Proceeding along the trans-Pacific line to San Francisco,—we are surprised that a detour was not made to the great Yosemite region, —the party had a pleasant time in the most wonderful city on that side of the Pacific, San Francisco, built, as it is, on land where thirty years ago the waves of the sea washed over a sandy shore. The story is told that it was no uncommon thing years ago for a carriage and pair of horses to fall through the roadway of the principal street of San Francisco, owing to the hurried and "scamped" work of the piling on which the "metal" (not the famous Californian yellow metal) was laid. Desiring to reach the Old World, a long sea-voyage of twenty-five days, even in a Pacific mail-boat going over twelve knots an hour throughout, was before the tourists, and the dismal forebodings of those who shared Dr. Johnson's views of traveling in ships were fully borne out in the drear monotony ("not a rock even to be seen from shore to shore") of the voyage, and the bad cooking of indifferent food which marked the cuisine of the Colorado, though it is only fair to the Pacific Mail Company to say that exceptional circumstances led to this result. Yokohama was the first port of call of the Colorado, and here the party landed, being favored during their whole stay with fine weather, though it was the time of " much rain," according to local meteorologists. All the principal sights of Japan were visited, the inland sea, Yeddo, Osaka, etc. A stay was made at Nagasaki, and the next land "made" was the " Flowery Land," Shanghai being the port of embarkation. A week's detention occurred here through losing the M. M. steamer, and at length passages were secured by the P. and O. steamer, which took them to Hong Kong, and they reached the latter port some days after the S. S. Japan (of the Pacific Mail line) had been burnt to the water's edge and sunk almost in sight of Hong Kong. Not unnaturally, the news of this disastrous event caused these roamers o'er land and sea a shadow of anxiety. A stay of two and a half days enabled the most active of the party to run up to Canton, where some of them were so enchanted with what they saw, and so desirous of "shopping" in the famous Chinese city, that they were left by their friends to come on in the Sindh, due at Galle on the Thursday following. The party express their great indebtedness to Archdeacon Gray of Hong Kong, who gave some of his time to cicerone the party, and did this so successfully that this was the most thoroughly "done" of all the places they visited. Brief stays were made at Singapore and Penang, the next halting-place being Ceylon.

As we have said, the more active of the party are now visiting the coffee districts; and after leaving Ceylon the whole company proceed to Madras and Calcutta, spending twenty-eight days in India. Egypt, from Cairo as a centre, will be gazed at, and the party will break up at Alexandria, where Mr. Cook has a large agency. Signor Caprani goes from Alexandria to take charge of a company for Palestine. Two of the party (besides the representative of Mr. Cook) are Italians; and Signor Caprani expresses the hope that this trip will demonstrate to many of his well-to-do countrymen how much better it would be for them to make "i giro del mondo a vapore," as the Italian circular of Messrs. Cook & Sons has it, than to find their recreation in the region of the cafés. We can only add that new Italy will be the better for the traveling of her sons.

CALCUTTA.

Calcutta, India, January 24, 1875.—Calcutta is about a hundred miles from the mouth of the Hoogly,—one of the outlets of the Ganges. The greater part of the distance up from the sea the banks of the river are a wild jungle, through which are scattered sometimes in groves the cocoanut and the palm, the whole vegetation having a strictly oriental aspect. The banks of the stream are as flat as those of the Lower Mississippi. Near the mouth of the Hoogly stands a monument, sad as a memorial, and strikingly suggestive of adventures which are still to be met with in all parts of India. It marks the spot where a young lady once disappeared in the grasp of a tiger. A vessel from home was detained by the tide, and a number of passengers concluded to go on shore and while away the time by a stroll among the palms. One of the party strayed a little from the rest, when a scream was heard; they ran to her assistance, but only in time to see her carried off by one of the tigers that still infest the jungles, even in the vicinity of the towns.

THE BANYAN.

About two miles below Calcutta, among many of the choice trees of the tropics, stands one of the finest specimens of the banyan-tree in all India; I do not know the number of its trunks, but one of these trees is described as having three hundred and fifty large branches that have shot down and become rooted, forming three hundred and fifty large trees and more than three thousand smaller ones, making from one tree, still joined together by its branches, an immense grove. We went to see it by carriage.

WATER SUPPLY.

The city is supplied with water from immense tanks, reservoirs of one or two hundred feet square sunk into the ground, but left entirely open. The natives walk down into them, bathe their bodies and wash their clothes, and then fill their jars or goat-skins with the water for drinking and other domestic uses. This is a specimen of native cleanliness.

The streets are watered by a truly oriental method. Each waterman has instead of a cart a goat-skin taken off entire, and forming an immense bottle left open at the neck; this is suspended by a strap over the shoulders of a coolie, who seizes the neck with one hand, and, as he walks along, deftly throws the water hither and thither. Large numbers of these coolies are kept constantly employed sprinkling the streets, which are as well watered by this method as by our own.

GOVERNMENT OF INDIA.

The European population of India, of whom the natives of the British Isles form by far the largest part, is about one hundred and sixty thousand. They are chiefly engaged in the public service, military and civil, although in the principal cities there is a large mercantile population.

During the hot season all business requiring active exertion is crowded as much as possible into the early morning, especially if it makes exposure to the sun necessary. The army-drill is over by eight or nine o'clock; traveling is done by night and during the middle of the day; the struggle for existence is most wisely managed by ceasing the struggle altogether, and giving one's self up to perfect quiet.

THE PUNKA.

The slightest exercise produces violent perspiration, and the same effect follows the suspension of the punka. The punka is a broad fan suspended overhead, and usually stretching across the room; in the dining-room, reaching the length of the table, it is moved by coolies in an anteroom, who, by means of a cord attached to the punka, draw it back and forth. Every private house, every place of business, and every assembly-room is supplied with this indispensable requisite. The churches have suspended over the heads of the congregation immense punkas, which wave back and forth majestically during the entire service. Rev. Mr. Hutton, missionary, says, "The first time that I was called upon to address a congregation through such a medium, I found it far less suggestive of ideas and suitable emotions than if I had been speaking to the people face to face." But even the heat of a church would be unendurable without the punkas. They are quite as essential at night in the homes during the hot season; no sleep can be had without them. Nor are they such a severe task upon the coolies as might be supposed. They are paid for the service, and it is their only support; they luxuriate in the heat as do the natives of Africa, and they have their time for rest: few natives of any country in the East die of hard work.

TEMPERANCE.

I have never been in any land where free indulgence within the bounds of temperance was more generally the rule. Foreign residents rise early all the year round, and take a cup of tea with toast or some light food immediately on rising; this is chotahazril or the little breakfast. About nine or ten o'clock comes the real breakfast, usually an elaborate meal of fish, eggs, and some preparation of rice, with meats: at one o'clock, taffin, a still more hearty meal, is taken; and at seven or eight o'clock, dinner, which is the meal of the day, and is much after the pattern of an English or American dinner. This generous style of living seems to agree with the people; for instead of the yellow- or dark-skinned, shrunken-livered, diseased race that I expected to see, I found the gentlemen robust and rosy-faced, to my great astonishment, and the ladies equally well-favored. They assured us that we found them at their best in the midst of the cool season, when they were luxuriating in a genial temperature; but from the general aspect of the foreign residents I felt convinced that India had been greatly belied, or that foreigners had learned to adapt themselves to its climate better than in years past.

HEAT.

I was informed by a gentleman who had resided near the Himalaya Mountains, on the plain, for thirty years, that he had often seen the thermometer for weeks standing at mid-day, in the shade, at one hundred and ten, one hundred and twenty, and one hundred and thirty degrees, and at night it seldom falls, during the hot season, below ninety or one hundred degrees. This would be almost insupportable but for the punkas, which are kept moving night and day.

The mountains and high table-lands afford a refuge, like the shadow of a great rock in a weary land, to those who are able to remove. In June, when the heat is at its greatest, the clouds pile up and the southeast monsoon bursts upon the land, attended with terrific storms of thunder and lightning and torrents of rain.

SAND-STORMS.

The sand-storms of India are even more remarkable than the rain: they are violent whirlwinds, occurring occasionally in the dry season, gathering up the dust and carrying it over the country in such volumes as actually to make midday as dark as midnight.

AMERICAN ICE.

One of the greatest luxuries in India is American ice, which at the principal ports is received in large quantities and is freely used. It comes from Boston, and is no inconsiderable item in the trade with Bombay and Calcutta. The price of ice at Bombay and Calcutta varies from two and a half to five cents per pound, according to the supply, and even at those rates it is accounted as indispensable to living as in American cities, and the luxury is inconceivably greater. If it is a blessing in America, where the thermometer sometimes reaches ninety-five degrees as the extreme heat of the day, what a boon must it be in the north of India, where for days and nights together the thermometer does not fall as low as one hundred degrees, and where it often reaches in the day one hundred and twenty and one hundred and thirty degrees! But the most of the people of India never see ice,—it is a miracle in their eyes.

CALCUTTA TO BOMBAY.

The route by rail from Calcutta to Bombay is, by way of Allahabad, a distance of one thousand four hundred and seventy miles; another two thousand two hundred miles was completed in March, 1870. Passengers from England to Calcutta and the cities up the valley of the Ganges had sailed direct from Calcutta by the Cape or through the Red Sea, but now they land at Bombay, where they take the rail to Allahabad, eight hundred and forty-five miles, and thence to Calcutta, six hundred and twenty-five miles, or to the North Indies, two thousand two hundred miles.

OPIUM.

Opium is produced in Bengal almost exclusively in a district lying along the Ganges, about six hundred miles long and two hundred miles broad. It is the dried juice of the capsules of the common white poppy, extracted before the seed is fully ripe. The poppy fields, when in full bloom, resemble green lakes studded with white water-lilies, the tract of country in which they grow being perfectly level.

THE NATIVES OF INDIA.

Native society! Why, there is no such thing. The women never see any one, and the men spend their time eating and sleeping. This is a strong statement, but with exceptional cases it is the truth. There is no social life among the native population of India. The woman is no society to her husband, the only man whom, as a rule, she ever meets; the man is no society for his wife; he regards her as belonging to an inferior order of beings, created to administer to his pleasure and comfort as a servant. There is nothing like social intercourse between brothers and sisters and outside of the family; society, in our understanding of the term, has no existence. Life is a dreary waste, judging by the standards which prevail in all countries with which we are familiar.

It is not for want of people that there is no society in India. Within the compass of one thousand nine hundred miles in one direction and one thousand five hundred in another, there are two hundred millions of people thrown together. The most numerous of these are the Hindoos, who compose about three-fourths of the population, or one hundred and fifty millions. Then come the Mohammedans, who number about twenty-five millions. The remaining eighth is made up of the aboriginal tribes, whose direct descendants still number several millions, the Parsees, the Buddhists, the Jews, and the Christians. The Hindoos are the grossest idolaters that ever existed; their forms of idol worship and service have reached the lowest degradation, and yet the Mohammedans, whose religion is essentially a protest against idolatry, have lived with them for long centuries, and each have maintained their own religion intact.

The traveler going into their bazaars and markets has his curiosity still more excited. Their habits and customs, so far as he is allowed to observe them, will keep awake all his powers of observation. The costumes of the Hindoos are the same that were worn centuries before the Christian era; that of the men usually consists of two pieces of wide cotton cloth, one of which is wrapped around the waist and falls to the calf of the leg, the other thrown loosely over the shoulder. A shawl or turban of some kind thrown upon the head completes the dress. The women have a single piece of cloth, silk or cotton, plain or colored, eight or ten yards long, which is first partly tied around the waist, forming a garment that reaches to the feet; the rest is then passed around the body and over the head, falling down the back; a tight bodice is frequently worn underneath. The dress, especially that of the women, has a graceful appearance, and, as the colors are often bright, a company together presents a striking appearance.

THE BRAHMINS.

The Brahmins eat no animal food of any kind, having a religious abhorrence of the destruction of life; some of them have the water they drink carefully strained, lest it should contain a gnat. Even eggs are forbidden, as possessing the germ of animal life. All Hindoos of every caste abstain from beef. Mohammedans, of course, eschew pork. Brahmins and others of high caste abstain from all intoxicating drinks, using only water or pure milk. The rules of caste are not broken by crime: a man may commit a murder, adultery, theft, or perjury, and even be convicted of such crimes, without losing caste; but if he violates any of the ceremonial laws, especially if he should eat with a European, even with a Mohammedan of India, or with any one not belonging to his class, he would be degraded, and only by the most humiliating process of atonement and by paying an enormous sum could he be restored at all. A Brahmin was once forced by a European to eat meat; although his offense was involuntary, he could not be restored after three years' penance even by the offer of forty thousand dollars' ransom. He subsequently regained his former position by the payment of one hundred thousand dollars' ransom. A while ago in India a high-caste Hindoo was present at an entertainment, partly social and partly official, given by Europeans, and partook of some articles of food in their society; he was afterwards compelled to pay a heavy fine, to eat the excrements of beasts, and to humble himself before an idol with costly presents before he could be recognized by those of his own caste.

THE GANGES.

Great numbers of Hindoos, men and women, have come down the long flights of steps to bathe in the Ganges, and all along we see them performing their ablutions with religious solemnities, hoping thus to wash away their sins; others are worshiping the river itself, bowing often and repeating their prayers, absorbed in their devotion, and apparently unconscious of the presence of others. Every now and then we come to a landing-place devoted to the burning of the Hindoo dead. We pass pile after pile made ready for the cremation; from some the smoke and flames are ascending to perfume the city, making this quarter of the town almost unendurable, excepting to a Hindoo.

BENARES TO ALLAHABAD.

The night is the time to travel in India at all seasons of the year. As there was little that was attractive in the scenery which we were to pass, we left Benares at the same time of the evening at which we had entered it. We crossed the Ganges in the beautiful moonlight, which spread a wondrously weird sheen over the massive monuments to the false prophets, and upon its thousand diminutive Hindoo temples and shrines along its magnificent banks. Were we in the mystical land of the Arabian Nights, or in the dream-land of the Hindoo Mythology?

BENARES.

In one respect Benares has a peculiar importance; it is the chief place of pilgrimage, and through the multitudes that gather here every year an influence may be sent out into every part of the land. Situated at the confluence of the two most sacred rivers of Hindostan, the Ganges and the Jumna, the spot is regarded by all Hindoos as one of the holiest places in the world. They come to it from all parts, and at all times of the year, to bathe where the two rivers meet, and thus to wash their sins away.

There is an annual mela or gathering at this place in the month of January, when hundreds of thousands come together, and every twelfth year, owing to some propitious conjunction of the stars, there is a special gathering, when the number of pilgrims is sometimes counted by millions. I had seen them far up the north the week before coming down in large companies; they continued to arrive at all hours of the day and night for days and even weeks, like a continuous procession. Some of the wealthier people came on elephants, others on camels, many of them, especially the aged and feeble, in carts drawn by bullocks or cows, but the most of them on foot, with the dust and dirt of their long pilgrimage upon them.

In the vast crowd were thousands of faquirs or devotees, who were almost naked and covered with dirt, their hair matted with filth, more disgusting in their appearance than swine, and accounting themselves all the more holy because of the excessive filth in which they had chosen to live.

Bathing in muddy streams and living in abominable filth seem to be the two leading articles in the creed of the Hindoos, at least of those who pretend to eminent holiness: the very reverse of the Christian maxim that cleanliness is a part of godliness. More abominable or more horrid specimens of human nature than these faquirs can scarcely be conceived, and the more painful part of it was that the poor ignorant people have been taught to regard these filthy, depraved brutes in human shape as pre-eminently holy.

Some of the devotees had made their pilgrimage all the way upon their hands and knees; others by dragging themselves along the ground, and one man, perhaps more, by measuring his length like an inch-worm, lying down, making a mark at his head, and then lying down with his toes at the mark, and so making his progress towards the consecrated spot; one man whom I saw at the mela had held his right hand above his head eleven years, and was, of course, accounted an eminent saint.

After the pilgrims have been shaven, and have bathed and performed other religious services, they devote themselves to social intercourse, to traffic, and often to all manner of wickedness, so that the mela becomes a mixed scene, the religious part bearing but a slight proportion to the whole.

I believe that the whole system of idolatry is now sustained more by the avarice of the Brahmins, who become wealthy from their perquisites, and by the incidental gains connected with it, than the religious feelings of the people. Priestcraft has a mighty power in keeping up rites which, if left to the choice even of ignorant people, would speedily come to an end.

AGRA AND TAJ.

About a mile to the south of the fort at Agra, upon the river Jumna, lies a beautiful park about a quarter of a mile square, planted with the choicest trees and shrubs and flowers of the East.

More than eighty fountains scattered along the avenues of this park throw their jets into the air, which sparkles with the falling drops as with a shower of diamonds. It is surrounded by a high wall, and guarded by a magnificent gateway, a building fifty or sixty feet in height, which, with any other surroundings, would be studied and admired for its architectural grandeur and the beauty of its carving and mosaic ornamentation. No one would imagine it to be simply the portal to greater beauty and grandeur, but such it is.

We enter beneath this majestic arch, and find ourselves within the park. A broad avenue, skirted with lofty cypresses, acacias, and other oriental trees, and tanks of aquatic plants and *jets d'eau*, reveals at its extremity an object which at once rivets the eye, and steals over the heart like a strain of delicious music or like the melody of sublime poetry; it is the Taj,—the peerless Taj,—the mausoleum erected by the Emperor Sha Jehan as the tomb of his favorite Begum, Noor Mahel, and in which they now sleep side by side. She died before him, in giving birth to a child; and it is stated that as she felt her life ebbing away she sent for the emperor, and told him she had only two requests to make: first, that he would not take another wife, and have children to contend with her's for his favor and dominions, and, secondly, that he would build the tomb for her that he had promised, to perpetuate her memory. The emperor summoned the medical counselors of the the city to do everything that was in their power to save her life, but all in vain.

Sha Jehan, who was devotedly attached to her, at once set about complying with her last request. The tomb was commenced immediately, and, according to Tavernier, who saw its first and last stones laid, it was twenty-two years being built, with twenty thousand men constantly employed upon it. It cost in actual expense, in addition to the forced labor of the men, more than three hundred lacs of rupees, or about fifteen million dollars. Such a building, including the cost of materials, could scarce be erected by paid labor at the present time, even in India, for fifty million dollars. This building is acknowledged by every traveler to be unrivaled, and the sight of it declared by many to be worth a journey around the world.

Let us enter, but breathe softly and tread gently as you step within. It is the sleeping-chamber, where lie, side by side, Noor Mahel and Sha Jehan, each on a couch of almost transparent marble, set with precious stones and wrought exquisitely in tracery of vines and flowers. Nowhere else has human dust been laid away to slumber in such superb repose,—so beautiful, so silent, so sacred, so sublime! In such perfect and exquisite taste is everything within, as well as without, that it is more like a creation than the work of man.

The whole interior, which is lighted only from the lofty doorway, is open from wall to wall and from the pavement to the summit of the dome, with the exception of a high marble screen standing about twenty or thirty feet from the outer wall, and extending entirely around the building. This is cut into open tracery, so as to resemble a curtain of lace rather than a screen of solid marble. The sarcophagi containing the remains of the empress and her faithful lover, the Mogul Emperor, lie in the crypt below, which is reached by a marble stairway. That of the former has inscribed upon it, in the graceful Arabic characters, "Moon taj i Mahel Ranoo Begum" (Ranoo Begum, the ornament of the palace), with the date of her death, 1631; the other has inwrought the name of the emperor, with the date of his death, 1666. To this day they are covered with fresh flowers, strewn by faithful hands in recognition of the fidelity which raised the structure.

The building, which was well filled, had no benches, the whole congregation, according to oriental custom, being seated on the floor, each one clothed in pure white, the women and girls with their long muslin garments drawn over their heads as veils, and all devoutly engaged in the service, joining in the responses and in prayer, bowing their foreheads to the pavement. The services were conducted in the Hindostanee tongue, and were unintelligible to us; but before us was a congregation of people who had been called out of the grossest idolatry, now devoutly engaged in worshiping the Saviour of the world, joining with Christians of all lands in the song of the heavenly host, "Glory to God in the highest, and on earth peace and good will toward men!"

This is one of the numerous scenes witnessed in India which show that the gospel of Christ, through the power of the Divine Spirit, is making its conquests, and giving promise of a day when it shall completely triumph over idolatry and superstition.

TOMB OF AKBAR.

The tomb of Akbar, one of the Mogul emperors, stands near Secundra, in the midst of a quadrangular court a quarter of a mile square; a heavy wall surrounds the square, making the inclosure a fortress. The mausoleum in which lie the remains of the great emperor is three hundred feet square, and vies in magnificence, though not in beauty, with the Taj, rising to the height of one hundred feet in five terraces, with the cloisters, galleries, domes, and cupolas elaborately wrought. Akbar was the most powerful sovereign of his day, and a man of independent if not enlightened views.

India is a perfectly level country. I could scarcely tell how the water ran. I could see ten miles from the railroad each way in passing along.

THE MUTINY.

But in no respect was I more struck with the diversity of sentiment among intelligent and well-informed people than in regard to the cause of the terrible mutiny of 1857, which came so near extinguishing the power of the English in the East. I doubt if any rebellion of equal extent and importance ever before occurred which could not be traced more directly and more clearly to its origin. At Allahabad the native regiment stationed at the town suddenly revolted, shot down the superior officers and bayoneted the younger, attacked the residents,—men, women, and children,—cutting them to pieces while alive. Children were tossed on the bayonets of the native soldiers before their mothers, and atrocities committed which the pen cannot record.

The remnant of the English who escaped took refuge in the fort, which was besieged by the sepoys. Having no fortress, they quickly intrenched themselves by throwing up earthworks on the open plain. The space they occupied was about two hundred yards square, and included a few small buildings. There were nine hundred persons in all within the narrow space. A murderous fire was opened upon them by the sepoys, which, with the famine, the burning sun of June, the close confinement, and other causes, told fearfully upon their numbers from day to day. Many died, and some went raving mad. At length the enemy began to pour upon them red-hot shot, which fired the buildings; the sick persons perished in the flames. While in this extremity they received an offer from the rebel leader, Nana Sahib, that if they would abandon the intrenchment and the treasures which they had been guarding, the survivors should be furnished with boats and an escort to take them down the Ganges to Allahabad. It was not until Nana Sahib had signed the contract, and confirmed his promise with a solemn oath, that the offer was accepted. Conveyance was provided for the wounded, the sick, and the feeble to the river, about a mile distant.

They were in the act of embarking, when, by order of Nana Sahib, a battery opened upon them, and numbers were slain. A few boat-loads hastily rowed across the river, but they were seized by the sepoys, the men all sabred, and the women and children carried back to the camp of the monster who had thus violated his oath. For weeks they were incarcerated in a building at Cawnpoor, where they were subjected to the brutality of the sepoy troops. At sunset on the 15th of July volleys of musketry were fired into the doors and windows of the building, after which the bayonet and sword did their work, until all were supposed to be dead, and the building was closed for the night.

The next morning it was found that a number were still alive, who, upon being brought out, either threw themselves or were thrown into a large well in company with the dead of the night before.

Thus perished all who had survived the slaughter of the Ghaut, nearly two hundred in all. The whole number of victims at Cawnpoor was about one thousand.

The army under Havelock entered Cawnpoor, the day after the massacre, driving out the rebels before them. And when they reached the building which was the scene of the massacre, and found it strewn with the relics of the departed ones,— remnants of clothing, ladies' and children's shoes, locks of hair, and other mementos, and the floor covered deep with their blood,—the brave soldiers were almost maddened by the sight.

CAWNPOOR.

On the plain at Cawnpoor is one of the most beautiful parks in the East,—laid out with exquisite taste, and planted with trees and shrubbery and ever-blooming flowers. In the midst of this park are the marble walls of a sacred inclosure, in the centre of which, over the fatal well, stands a marble statue,—an angel, having in his arms the palm-leaves, emblematical of martyrdom and victory.

This park was laid out and planted after the mutiny, and called the Memorial Garden; but it seemed designed as much to mitigate by its beauty as to preserve by its monuments the memories of the spot. The pedestal on which stands the angel bears the following inscription: "Sacred to the memory of a great number of Christian people, chiefly women and children, who, near this spot, were cruelly massacred by the followers of the rebel Nana Dhoonduphunt, of Bithoor, and cast, the dying with the dead, into the well below, on the 15th of July, 1857."

While General Wheeler and his command, with his precious charge, were still in their frail intrenchment, the mutiny broke out at Futtehgunge, higher up the Ganges. This has long been one of the chief stations of the American Protestant Missions in India. All the mission-buildings, including a valuable printing-office, were destroyed. The foreign residents were put to the sword, the English officers and civilians being the first to suffer. The survivors, including four American missionary families, attempted to escape in boats, hoping to reach Allahabad. The Americans were Rev. Messrs. Freeman, Johnson, Campbell, and McMullen, with their wives and two children of Mr. Campbell.

The large party, one hundred and thirty in all, floated down the Ganges, all the while in terror of the natives; twice they were fired upon, and a lady, nurse, and child were killed. Once they landed at evening to cook some food on shore; they were surprised by Ziminder, who made them his prisoners, but they were released on the payment of a large ransom.

On the fourth day the boats ran aground near an island, a few miles above Cawnpoor. The whole party went ashore, and concealed themselves in the long grass, where they remained in constant apprehension of discovery, and with little hope of escape. In this hiding-place they assembled for prayer and preparation for death, the missionaries leading them to the throne of God's mercy to seek grace for the hour of greater trial that awaited them, and exhorting every one to steadfastly trust in Him, who would bring salvation even in death.

The record of these solemn scenes was derived from four native Christians, who were the only survivors. Near the close of the fourth day they were discovered by a body of sepoys, who came upon the island, made them prisoners, and, deaf to all appeals for mercy and offers of ransom, took them across the river on the way to Cawnpoor. Though exhausted by long fasting and anxiety, they were tied together with ropes, and men, women, and children compelled to take up the line of march on foot. Night overtaking them, it was spent on the plain in the open air, the sepoys keeping guard over them to prevent their escape.

Early next morning they were taken into Cawnpoor to Nana Sahib, who ordered them to be drawn up in line on the parade ground, where they were indiscriminately shot down; those who survived the volley of musketry were dispatched with the sabre. When they were first seized by sepoys, the missionaries dismissed the four native Christians, advising them to seek their own safety, but under no circumstances to deny their Lord and Master. One of them, a man who had been a servant to the Maharajah Dhuleepsingh, disguised himself, followed the captive party, and was a witness to the last fearful scene in which their lives were offered up. From him the knowledge of their fate was obtained.

DELHI.

The vicinity of Delhi is a field in which the antiquarian may revel in endless delight. Within a circle of twenty miles one dynasty after another has established its capital and ruled in splendor, and then passed away, leaving the field to the conqueror, who, instead of occupying the same site, has founded a new city and left the old one to crumble into ruins. In this way numerous cities have been scattered over the plain, the monuments of some remaining to this day, while the very history of others has been lost. One monument, the loftiest single column in the world, stands about ten miles from Delhi, of the magnificent ruins of which there is no satisfactory account in the records of India. Old Delhi, as it is called, the last forsaken site, is in greater perfection; the walls remain, and much of the city is yet standing, but its halls are deserted, and vagabonds and beasts of prey share its hospitality alike.

But if the region is a field for the antiquarian, the present city, for a long time the capital of the Mogul Empire, is the home of fancy and the field of romance. Delhi was founded by the Sha Jehan about two centuries and a half ago. One principal street, the Chandnee Chowk, one hundred and twenty feet wide, divides the town, and is daily the scene of more strictly Asiatic display than any other street in India. It is alike the Boulevard and the Broadway of Delhi. On either side are the shops and warehouses of the wealthy merchants; the centre is a broad terrace or promenade, shaded with acacias and other ornamental trees. During the day the Chandnee Chowk is a busy mart of trade; but towards evening the loaded trains of camels and other beasts of burden disappear, the hum of business dies away, and a scene of oriental leisure and display ensues. The promenade is thronged with persons in all the varied costumes of the interior of Asia, while richly-caparisoned Arabian horses, elephants with gayly-dressed riders, and not a few English carriages belonging to the natives, pass up and down the street.

Other parts of the city are equally curious in their way. The grain markets are among the sights; camels and buffaloes, with their heavy freights, come and go like ships entering and leaving port, and a noisy multitude, scarcely less bewildering and far more entertaining than the crowd of a Western exchange, almost fascinates the stranger.

We were taken to see an immense well, eighty-five feet in depth and about fifty feet in diameter. A half dozen nearly-naked natives stood around the edge waiting for the nod that seals the contract to pay them for the exploit. We nodded, and at once they sprang with outstretched arms and legs, and kept in this position until within about twenty feet of the bottom, when they suddenly straightened themselves, plunging feet foremost into the water, and soon reappeared swimming on its surface. They speedily reached the top by an underground passage and demanded their pay, and would not have been satisfied if we had given them ten times the usual amount; but it is their only means of support, and they, as well as their fathers before them for many generations, and perhaps for centuries, have followed plunging into the same well from their childhood.

MASSACRE AT DELHI.

The revolt commenced at Meerut, forty-nine miles distant, and after the massacre of the Europeans, men, women, and children, at that place, the sepoys set out in a body for Delhi, where the native troops joined them, and commenced the slaughter of their officers. The magazine, which contained an enormous supply of guns, powder, and other warlike stores, was in charge of Lieutenant Willoughby. Seeing the state of affairs, he closed and barricaded the gates, and then, laying a train of powder, prepared to blow up the arsenal should resistance prove unavailing. Nine Europeans kept thousands of sepoys at bay until at length they were exhausted and likely to be overpowered, when the match was applied, and more than a thousand mutineers were blown into the air. All the Europeans in the city who had not made their escape were massacred on the appearance of the sepoys. The English families were tied in rows and shot and sabred without mercy; the assassinations were accompanied by horrid atrocities. Others who escaped, tender women and helpless children, wandered for days under the burning sun, lying down at nights in the jungle. Delhi fell completely into the hands of the mutineers; but its recapture was one of the most heroic achievements of the recovery of British power in India.

SNAKES.

The most deadly and dreaded of the snakes is the hooded cobra, which sometimes attains the length of ten feet. There are also innumerable venomous snakes no larger than a riding-whip. It is stated on good authority that in the year 1869 there were eleven thousand four hundred and sixteen deaths from the bites of snakes in the single province of Bengal. From actual statistics it has been estimated that in all India there are twenty thousand to forty thousand deaths from the same cause every year. They live and multiply not only in the open country, but in the villages and cities. They come into the grounds and houses of all classes; they make their homes in the thatch and drop down from the rafters; they creep into the beds; they get among the kitchen utensils, and even ensconce themselves in the parlors. I heard many thrilling narratives of adventures with these unwelcome visitors; the smaller vermin are still more ubiquitous and a still greater annoyance. Scorpions and centipedes are abundant, and everywhere the white ants move in armies and are terribly destructive. Scarcely anything in the shape of furniture or clothing escapes their ravages, and their tastes are decidedly literary. They will "go through" an entire library in an incredibly short space of time, leaving nothing to be perused by those who come after them. If a book is carelessly left within their reach, the form of it may be found, but the entire contents will have been destroyed.

BOMBAY.

My observations have convinced me that this is destined to be the great city of India, if not of the whole Eastern world. In its general aspect, Bombay is the most lively city of the Indies. Its population, of nearly a million of people, is very multifarious. Nearly all the tribes of Hindostan are represented. Hindoos, Mussulmen, Parsees, Indo-Britons, Indo-Portuguese, Europeans of various nations, Americans, and natives of Western Asia. The costumes of the people are varied, and gay beyond description. The streets are thronged by a very busy multitude, on foot, on horseback, and in carriages, many of the latter gaudily trimmed and drawn by bullocks. Their dress is peculiar, partly European and partly oriental. They have a sort of caste, and are forbidden to marry excepting among their own people; nor do they usually eat what has been cooked by one of another religion. A well-educated Parsee and his wife were among our companions when crossing the Pacific Ocean. They mingled freely with the other passengers, and ate at the same table with them. On returning to Bombay he was called to account for violating the rules of his race, and his situation became so uncomfortable in consequence that he moved to London to take charge of a branch of the house with which he is connected.

The Parsees have a large cemetery on Malabar Hill, near Bombay; the highest ground in the vicinity is selected, so that no one can look into it. It contains a building devoted to the preservation of the sacred fire, besides buildings for the priests and for those who have charge of the dead.

Five round stone towers, each about fifty feet in diameter and forty or fifty in height, are the receptacles for the dead. When a death occurs, the body is taken to the gate of the cemetery and delivered into the hands of the priests. No one is allowed to enter the walls with the dead. After a prescribed ceremony the body is taken to one of the towers and laid upon a grate upon the top of it. A number of hideous vultures are always waiting to devour the flesh, and the bones fall into the body of the tower below in an indiscriminate heap. It is the most revolting mode of disposing of the remains of departed friends of which I have any knowledge, but the Parsees adhere to it with a tenacity which borders on fanaticism.

The Hindoo mode of disposing of the dead is far less repulsive. Across the bay, on the Bombay side, a row of brilliant lights stretched along the shore in the deep stillness of the night, and in the strangeness of the whole scene they had a mysterious look. On inquiry I learned that they were the funeral piles on which the Hindoos were burning their dead; being a more becoming mode of treating the remains of the departed—returning ashes to ashes—than the horrid funeral rites of the Parsees.

ADEN.

When once off the coast, the voyage through the Indian Ocean as far as Aden, seventeen hundred and sixty miles, was without any striking incident. A strong northeast monsoon kept our ship steady, helped us on our course, and supplied us with plenty of fresh air, a great blessing in those eastern seas. On the morning of the sixth day the shores of Arabia were in sight, and towards evening we descried the heights of Aden, ninety miles to the east of the entrance to the Red Sea. It is a mass of rock, connected with the main land by a low sandy neck, and towering up to the height of seventeen hundred and seventy-six feet. It was held by the Portuguese when they were stretching their arms and their commerce into the East. It was captured by the Turks in 1538, and held for three centuries; but in 1839, for an outrage committed upon a vessel sailing under the English colors, the

British Government seized the place, strengthened its fortifications, and have kept a large garrison upon it ever since. It is called the " Gibraltar of the East," on account of its commanding position near the entrance of the Red Sea and its great natural strength as a fortress.

Owing to some peculiarity in its situation it seldom rains at Aden, three or four years or even more sometimes passing without a drop falling from the clouds, even when it rains on the mainland near by.

THE RED SEA.

Passing through the Straits of Bab-el-Mandeb (the gate of tears or the gate of desolation as it is variously interpreted), we entered the Red Sea, which in all ages has been a terror to navigators. This narrow strip of water covers a small space on the map, but it is more than twelve hundred miles in length, making a voyage of five or six days by steam, during which the shore is seldom seen on either side. Its navigation is difficult and perilous; the water is of great depth, but rocks and islands are scattered through it, and coral reefs abound, which seldom lift their heads above the waves to warn the sailor of his danger. The shores are almost entirely destitute of lighthouses, and are occupied by inhospitable races of men where inhabited at all. High winds prevail during a great part of the year, making the navigation particularly undesirable for sailing vessels, which are now seldom seen.

Two or three days before entering Suez we encountered a fierce north wind, which never subsided until we were on shore. Every few minutes, on the last day or two of the voyage, a heavy sea would break over the bow of the ship, washing the deck from stem to cabin, while the cold blasts from the north drove us all under shelter, and many to their berths. How we came safely through we never knew, excepting that we had the guidance and protecting care of the great Pilot who holds the winds and the waters in the hollow of his hand.

It was not until the evening of the sixth day after our entering the straits, and the twelfth after our leaving Bombay, that we dropped anchor at Suez,—it may have been upon one of the chariot-wheels of Pharaoh. The sun had set before we reached the anchorage, which is five miles from the head of the gulf and from town. It was the same land over which, more than thirty-six centuries before, Moses led the children of Israel. The same sands were still there, though the footprints of the departing host had been obliterated; the same sea rolled before us; the same mountains frowned from the southwest; the general aspect of the scene was unchanged.

There is no doubt in regard to the route by

which they came from Succoth to the sea. The path is clearly defined by the features of the country. A precipitous mountain range stretches diagonally to the northwest, leaving a sandy plain between it and the sea, from which they could not diverge. All this was so clear that, as I looked over the vast plain, I could almost imagine I saw the great host on their march, the pillar of cloud leading them on by day, and the great curtain hung up by the hand of God to protect them from their pursuers by night.

But where was the point at which they heard the command of God to "go forward," and were so marvelously delivered from their enemies? Everything in the Divine record shows that they were forced to enter the bed of the sea at the spot on which they stood when the Lord said unto Moses, "Wherefore criest thou unto Me? Speak unto the children of Israel that they may go forward; but lift thou up the rod, and stretch out thine hand over the sea and divide it, and the children of Israel shall go on dry ground in the midst of the sea."

From an examination of these localities it appeared to me much more probable that they followed the sandy plain to the south, where the sea and the precipitous mountain range converge, and where it was impossible for them to move excepting in one direction. Pharaoh and his hosts were in their rear. They had fled until they could flee no farther,—a mountain wall was upon one side and the deep sea upon the other. God divided the waters before them, and they passed through the midst of the sea.

At the point to which I refer, the Red Sea must be five or six miles in width and of great depth; but the whole account indicates that the crossing took place where the sea was wide: the Egyptians, pursuing the Israelites, went in after them to the midst of the sea, even all Pharaoh's horses, his chariots, and his horsemen. It was in the midst of the sea that they proposed to turn back when they found the Lord was fighting for the Israelites against the Egyptians. They turned and fled, but when the sea came back to its bed, of the vast army that had gone into it there remained not so much as one of them. The simple narrative, the song of Moses, which he sang with the children of Israel to celebrate their deliverance, the allusions to it in other parts of the Holy Scriptures, show that it was a sublime miracle not accomplished by a concurrence of ordinary means, and therefore that there was no occasion for selecting a place where it could be easily performed, but rather the contrary.

The drying up of the waters was not effected alone by the strong east wind, for the children of Israel went into the midst of the sea upon the dry ground, and the waters were a wall unto them on their right hand and on their left. In the song of Moses it is said, "The floods stood upright as an heap, and the depths were congealed in the heart of the sea." This is not all poetic imagery.

SUEZ.

Suez is not an insignificant town. It has a population of several thousand, its bazaars are well supplied with goods for oriental consumption, and there is more of an air of activity and business about it than one might expect in such a desert region. When the overland route to India was opened a few years since, Suez had a revival of the traffic it enjoyed before the discovery of the route to the Indies by the Cape of Good Hope, but the more recent opening of the Suez Canal may be another blow to its prosperity, by making all transshipment of passengers and goods needless.

We were going down to the valley of the Nile by the same route which Abraham took when he went into Egypt to escape famine, by which the sons of Jacob went down to buy corn, and by which the grand funeral procession returned bearing the body of the patriarch to its resting place in the cave of Machpelah, where I have no doubt it still slumbers undisturbed.

CAIRO.

Here we caught sight of Cairo. Its golden light streamed over the domes and minarets, pouring itself in a flood upon the green fields and among the palms, and drawing a beautiful contrast between the buildings and the dark foliage in which they were set. The citadel with its grand mosque towered above the rest of the city, having for its background the gray mountains and the mausoleum of long-buried generations. The broad valley of the Nile, dressed in living green, was spread out before us.

They have strange chambermaids at Shepheard's Hotel, in Cairo. The one who waited on our room, and attended to all the various duties of the calling, even to the making of beds, was a courtly Frenchman, dressed as if for a dinner-party, and having the air of a refined and educated gentleman. It was really embarrassing to accept his services. One of the ladies on arriving at the hotel rang for the chambermaid. The gentleman presented himself. Supposing him to be the proprietor or chief clerk, she informed him that she had rung for the chambermaid. He very politely replied, in the best English he could command, "Madame, I am she."

My second expedition to Cairo, after recovering from the fatigue of our long voyage and subsequent journeyings by land, was to the Citadel itself, or the Grand Mosque, noted for the panoramic view of the city and of the valley of the Nile which it commands. This view alone would repay a traveler for coming to this far-off country, even if he should see nothing else. As you stand upon the parapet, the whole of Cairo, ancient and modern, lies at your feet. On the right are the tombs of caliphs and Mamelukes, on the left is what remains of old Cairo, called old by courtesy among the monuments of thirty or forty centuries. Beyond the city flows the Nile, encircling several beautiful islands. Farther on across the emerald valley sit the Pyramids and the Sphinx in silent majesty. A few miles up the Nile is the site of ancient Memphis, now nearly obliterated; below, where Joseph and Mary, resting themselves, sat under the sycamore tree. The hills on either side of the broad valley rising up as walls, seeming to say to the overflowing stream, "Thus far shalt thou come and no farther," are inhabited by a silent multitude —unnumbered millions—unknown and undecayed, who await the coming of the resurrection morn just as they were laid in their tombs thousands of years ago. In the midst of this scene the old Nile flows and overflows as it has from the time of the Pharaohs and from the time of the flood, if not from all time.

But we had expected to go up the Nile. Arrangements were therefore made for a trip of about seven hundred miles; but as we had traveled much farther than we expected to, passing through many cities of which I give no account, we gave up the project.

I gave you an account of Cairo, Egypt, two years ago, and don't want to speak more about it. We expect to go from Cairo to Alexandria, where we landed two years ago, and where they put us in prison for six days with nothing of any account to eat. I do most mortally hate Alexandria. But we will not stay here long, as we sail from Alexandria for Brindisi, Italy.

ALEXANDRIA.

Alexandria, the seaport and commercial capital of Egypt, contains about two hundred and fifty thousand inhabitants. The buildings come into view one by one. The tall column that first attracts the stranger's view is known as Pompey's Pillar. The city was founded by Alexander the Great three hundred and thirty-two years before Christ. Alexandria has two parts: that on the west, which is the best, is called the Old Harbor, that on the east the New. The population is very mixed, consisting, besides the native Turks and Arabs, of Americans, Greeks, Syrians, Maltese, Jews, and Europeans of almost every nation, in such numbers that it may be questioned whether the strangers you notice in the streets would not be more than a match for the natives.

POMPEY'S PILLAR.

The name given to this column is without historical foundation. The Greek inscription found upon it proves it to have been erected by Publius,

Prefect of Egypt, in honor of Diocletian, who besieged Alexandria two hundred and ninety-seven years after Christ. After eight months' defense the city was obliged to capitulate, when thousands were massacred by fire and sword. The height of the pillar, including the shaft, capital, and pedestal, is one hundred feet. It is of polished red granite, elegant, and in good style. But the capital and pedestal are inferior and unfinished.

CLEOPATRA'S NEEDLES.

These two obelisks may be seen in the eastern part of the city, near the shore; the one standing, the other lying down and nearly covered with earth. They are of red granite, and formerly stood before the Temple of Neptune at Heliopolis. One of them is sixty-five feet high, the other seventy. Their diameter at the base is eight feet. They were quarried in the reign of Thoth III., fourteen hundred and ninety-six years before Christ, and are consequently now thirty-three hundred and sixty-three years old. Mehemet Ali gave the fallen one to the British Government, but they concluded it was hardly worth the money it would cost to remove it. There is one at Rome, and one on the Place de la Concorde, Paris, very similar, and of the same stone.

BRINDISI.

We reached Brindisi after a very boisterous voyage. The ship was tossed upon the uneasy sea as a thing of no account. We tried to prepare ourselves as well as we could to withstand the blast, but we could not long keep the upper deck, and were forced to go to the cabin and take our berths, and even there we were not safe. At short intervals all day and night one crash after another was heard, as a stand broke loose or the steward's dishes went into a heap. Though in a mighty ship, we felt how weak are the proudest works of man in contending with the breath of the Almighty. We committed ourselves to his care. The waves tossed us up and down, and many of the passengers and sailors were sea-sick. Some of the passengers thought we would never reach Brindisi, but that the ship would go down in the sea, as the waves went over the ship time and again; but it stood the hurricane, and we landed in Brindisi safely. The ship was in the storm two days and two nights, and then the sea became calm.

The ancient Brentesion, signifying stag's head, so called from the closing tendency of arms of the harbor, has the principal hotel, De l'Orient, near the harbor. It is generally supposed that Brindisi was founded by Diomedes. It was in ancient times a place of considerable importance, being in the time of the Romans the point of embarkation from Italy to Greece. It then boasted of sixty thousand inhabitants. Polonius was born and Virgil died here. At Brindisi, Tancred's son,

Roger, was united in marriage to Irene, the daughter of the Grecian Emperor. About this time the fleets of the Crusaders frequently made Brentesion their stopping place. In 1348 the city was plundered and the inhabitants put to the sword by King Louis of Hungary. In 1416 a frightful earthquake destroyed nearly the whole city, and a great population. In 1845 it became a free port. Since its connection by rail with the east of Europe it has rapidly become a town of importance, being now the point of embarkation of travelers going to different ports on the Mediterranean.

Brindisi is, or was, the termination of the celebrated Via Appia, so often mentioned by different Latin poets and historians. Horace speaks of his journey to Brindisi by this road. The principal object of interest in the town is the castle built by Frederick II. and finished by Charles XII.

The environs of Brindisi are very unhealthy, owing to the marshes surrounding the town.

NAPLES.

We arrived at Naples at eleven o'clock P.M. on the 19th of March, 1875. I know of no other portion of Italy, unless it be the plain of Sardinia, that bears the marks of such fertility, or of such careful cultivation, as the region north of Naples. It is a vast garden. The soil is rich and easily tilled, and every road is improved. The trees are trimmed far up, destroying their beauty to a great degree, but letting in the sun and air upon the fields, while the vines are festooned from tree to tree above the growing crops, giving the country a holiday aspect.

The peasantry of Italy belong to a different race from the dwellers in the towns: they are more industrious in their habits; and large sections of the country, devoted to corn and the vine, attest their thrift.

In entering Naples one is struck with the vagabond, and at the same time lively, character of the mass of the people: they swarm there like bees just ready to desert a hive that has become too close to contain them. They live in the open air, not only seeking their amusements and attending to their ordinary business out of doors, but cooking in the very thoroughfares of the city. All seem bent on catching the pleasures of the day, as if there was no to-morrow.

Formerly the beggars constituted one of the most striking features of Neapolitan street-life: they were your escort on entering the city, coming out in crowds, sometimes for miles, to meet the public conveyance: they were unremitting in their attentions as long as you stayed, never failing to take off their hats whenever you made your appearance in the streets; and when you were leaving they followed you out of town, wishing you every blessing by all the saints if you answered their demands, and cursing you by the whole calender if you did not. Many of them had a merry way of begging : throwing somersaults, playing a tune upon their chins, or cutting antics to attract attention, like the merriest creatures alive; when they would tell you as the next thing that they were dying of hunger, and ask you for a little money for the love of the Madonna. The whole kingdom of Naples, and, for aught I know, adjacent kingdoms, had been raked and scraped to gather in the halt, the maimed, the lame, and the blind, and all the miserable and disgusting objects that could be found, as so much capital on which to drive the thriving trade of beggary, one of the principal branches of business in Naples, and not the least profitable either. But that is now changed, and one can go in and out of Naples and stay there with comparatively little annoyance from this source.

The Bay of Naples I regard as beyond comparison the finest single view in the world; it has a combination of beautiful features and of interesting associations that cluster around no other spot; the bay itself has a graceful sweep of thirty or forty miles within the islands placed at its mouth as sentinels to ward off the towering waves that come rolling in from the sea; its waters are almost as blue as the vault of the sky above it. At the centre of its broad sweep stands the genius of the scene, the beautiful, majestic, living mountain that has no equal; graceful in its outlines and standing alone in its grandeur like Fusiyama, the glory and pride of Japan. No other mountain has for my eye such a power of fascination; I have never looked about it, from whatever point or how often soever, that it has not had the same strange fresh interest as if I had never seen it before. It seems to be a living thing; there it stands year after year gently breathing out its vapor like breath, that floats away and is soon dissipated upon the frosty air. When in a state of eruption the signs of life are far more striking.

VESUVIUS.

The top of Vesuvius is the best point from which to take in the beauties of the bay and its surroundings. To the west lie the islands that form an important element in the perfection of the view. To the south are Sorrento and other sunny towns, with the blue mountains towering up behind them. The bright, gay city of Naples stretches for miles along the shore to the north. In the distance stands the tomb of Virgil, and farther on the town of Pozzuoli, the ancient Puteoli, the terminus of the Appian Way, at which Paul landed on his memorable journey to Rome when he appealed to Cæsar's judgment. Farther on are Baiæ and Conræ, the summer resorts of the Roman Emperors and of men of wealth,—the Newport of those days when they erected splendid palaces and reveled in luxury and display. The ruins of their magnificent summer palaces, which were built out into the sea and overhung the heights, stretch for miles along the shores. From these same shores and surroundings Virgil took the scenery of his Æneid. Here are Lake Avernus and the river Styx and the Elysian Fields; here too are the Sibyls' Caves. No part of Italy, not even Rome itself with its suburbs, was more consecrated by the homes and writings of her emperors, orators, and bards.

HERCULANEUM.

At the foot of Vesuvius lie the long-buried citizens of Herculaneum and Pompeii, revealed to-day after slumbering forgotten for eighteen centuries. A world of interest gathers around them as we look down into the silent, deserted streets that were so long filled with a bustling crowd, and then in one dark storm were overwhelmed.

In what part of the world can so much that is beautiful in scenery, so much that is fraught with classic interest, and so much that stirs the heart with tragic recollections be seen at a single glance, as from the heights of this burning mountain? and this is an indication of the manner in which the traveler may occupy his time and his attention in his sojourn at the sunny city of Naples.

It requires many days to make the various excursions, but I shall not attempt the task of conducting the reader through all of them.

Vesuvius was a burning mountain two thousand years before the Christian era. Its fires were extinguished and slumbered for a while; but just about the time that Paul landed at Puteoli it was again seized with convulsions, the whole region was violently shaken, and several towns were laid in ruins.

POMPEII.

The memorable eruption in which Herculaneum and Pompeii were overwhelmed,—the former by lava, and the latter by the shower of ashes,—occurred in the year 79 A.D. The younger Pliny, who witnessed it, states that about one o'clock in the day he saw a strange cloud overhanging the plain of Naples like a huge pine-tree, shooting up to a great height and stretching out its branches; this singular cloud, which seemed to be composed of earth and cinders, excited his curiosity, and he embarked in a boat to cross the bay and examine into it: as he approached the coast the red-hot cinders and stones fell into the boat, and he was obliged to retreat. He proceeded to Stabiæ to spend the night with a friend, but before morning they were driven to the fields by the shaking of the house. The morning came, but it brought no relief; one shock of earthquake succeeded another, as if the foundations of the world were giving way; the sea receded from the shore, the mountain poured forth a mass of flame and burning rock, and the cloud of cinders spread over the bay and the land: they attempted again to escape to a safer distance, and joined the crowd that was surging onward. Pliny's father having already perished, he led his mother by the hand, and, fearing she would be pressed to death, proposed to step aside and suffer the crowd to pass by. He says he had scarce stepped out of the path when darkness overspread them,—not like that of a cloudy night, or when there is no moon, but of a room when it is shut up and all the lights are extinguished. Nothing was to be heard but the screams of children for their parents, and of women for their husbands, who were only to be distinguished by their voices: one lamenting his own fate, another that of his family; some wishing to die from the fear of dying, some lifting their hands to the gods; but the greater part imagining that the last and eternal night was come which was to destroy the gods and the world together. This was the most fearful eruption on record; many of less account have since occurred, the most remarkable in 1779, in which, according to Sir William Hamilton, the molten lava was thrown in jets to the height of ten thousand feet. More than once have the sides of the mountain broken in while the melted lava poured out of its sides and ran in streams toward the plain below.

In 1851, I made the ascent of the mountain, reaching the top of the cone, and looking down into the abyss. It was then comparatively quiet, but the presage of a coming explosion was noticeable.

I was on Vesuvius three times since 1851, but no eruption occurred while I was there.

Herculaneum was buried too deep in solid lava ever to be excavated to any great extent; but the larger part of Pompeii has been reclaimed, and one may now walk for miles through its streets and among its buildings. He need not lose his way, many of the streets having the names upon the corners, as in modern cities.

The ancient pavement, rutted deep by the carriage-wheels, remains intact; not equal, it is true, to the Belgian, but as firm as when it was laid eighteen centuries ago. Entering the homes of the Pompeians as they were discovered, we find in them bracelets and jewels, some of exquisite workmanship, gold and precious stones. Here are writing materials, ink-stands and pens, lamps as they went out when Pompeii was extinguished, thimbles, distaffs, and spinning-wheels; in short, the whole catalogue of a woman's domestic life, together with all the paraphernalia of the toilet, even the rouge and false hair.

The cellars were stored with wine, and although the old Falernian has long since evaporated, the amphoræ or earthen jars which contained the wine stand in rows along the walls. In the house of Diomede, one of the most extensive and elaborately-ornamented villas, situated near one of the gates of the city, were large numbers of wine-jars of great size. This house, being remote from the centre of the town, was evidently resorted to by the friends of the owner as a place of comparative safety, but more persons probably lost their lives in it than in any other. The skeletons or forms of seventeen persons were found in the cellars. On the women were found gold necklaces and bracelets and other ornaments. Two little children, whose heads were still covered with beautiful hair, were found.

In one of the houses of Pompeii two of the bodies are kept in a glass case, the attitudes and posture of the limbs expressing the mortal agony which came upon them. Diomede himself was found near the garden-gate with a purse of gold and other valuables in his hand, while an attendant stood by his side grasping the key to the gate. Some of the houses have the names of the owners inscribed on the outer wall, especially those of a more imposing character. Among the familiar names is that of C. Sallust. The house of Pansa thus marked, one of the largest in the city, contained five skeletons when it was opened. The shops with their contents are as great a curiosity as their homes. Some of them are extensive, and were the property of wealthy citizens, who derived their incomes from them. There are several bakeries or cook-shops in perfect preservation, from which large quantities of viands have been taken; in some the bread was found standing in the ovens. The notices around the doors and in the interior show that the art of advertising is not a modern invention. In one of the villas was found the following poster:

"Julius has to let for five years a Bath, a Venexium, Ninety Shops, with Terraces and upper Chambers."

They are still without tenants, although they have been advertised one thousand eight hundred years.

Nearly everything found in the shops and houses at Pompeii is preserved in the National Museum at Naples, one of the most interesting collections of antiquities in the world. By its help we can readily furnish the luxurious but now deserted homes, see how their inmates lived, and learn more of their domestic history than from any other source. One can study and muse for days over this extraordinary collection, and find his interest growing deeper every hour that he lingers.

Before leaving Naples we drove to the cities of

its own dead, as being among the characteristic features of the place. The Protestant cemetery is a neat churchyard in the outskirts of the town. The cypress here waves over the grave of many a stranger who has died far away from the friends and scenes of home. Flowers also bloom profusely in this sweet resting-place of those who have no more seas to cross and no farther journey in life to make.

CAMPO SANTO VECCHIO.

After lingering to note by the various inscriptions from how many lands the sleepers had come, we drove to the Campo Santo Vecchio, the great charnel-house of Naples. It contains three hundred and sixty-five pits, under a wide paved square. Every evening the stone which covers one of these pits is removed, and the common dead of the city for the day are thrown into it without even a winding-sheet to cover them. The old man and the child, the rough lazzaroni and the tender maiden, are dropped in together, and lie in one indiscriminate mass. Quick-lime is thrown in to consume the bodies, and the pit is sealed for another year, to be opened at its close. We did not wait to witness the revolting scene, although the city carts were arriving with the dead, but drove to the Campo Santo Nuovo, the cemetery for the aristocratic dead, and here I was surprised to find a burial-ground laid out with refined taste, shaded with cypress and other trees, and adorned with tombs of the most costly description. Many of them were in the form of chapels, built of fine Italian marble, elaborately finished.

After what I heard of the burial of the dead, and what I had seen at the Campo Vecchio, it was a relief to enter one that indicated so much refinement of feeling.

ROME.

We arrived at Rome March 22, 1875, at eleven o'clock at night. The next day we had Mr. Wood to take six carriages and conduct forty-four of Cook & Sons' party through every part of Rome. In four days I have seen more of Rome than I ever saw before. First we visited St. Peter's. Before the era of railways the traveler, in approaching Rome across the Campagna, was generally electrified by the first glimpse of St. Peter's dome looming in the distance, then had full time in advance of entering the gates of the city to ponder over all the recollections which the magical word Rome might suggest; at present he is rapidly borne into the city by moonlight, seeing everything, and sometimes before he is aware of even having arrived in its neighborhood; yet the dome is plainly visible from afar by the railway approach of to-day. Now, as then, the first sight of Rome is always her unequaled cathedral, the first object which the traveler hastens to visit. The present church of St. Peter's is relatively modern, having been first conceived by Pope Nicholas, about the year 1450. It is built upon the site of the religious edifice erected by Constantine, and consecrated by him as the Basilica of Saint Peter; the old Basilica stood on part of the Circus of Nero, and was supposed to occupy the spot consecrated by the blood of the martyrs slaughtered by order of the tyrant. Tradition supposes that it held possession of the body of the apostle after he was crucified,—a circumstance which reflected high credit upon it. After enjoying the veneration and tributes of all Christendom during eleven centuries, the walls of the old Basilica began to give way, and its approaching ruin becoming visible, about the year above stated Nicholas V. conceived the project of taking down the old church and erecting in its stead a new and more expensive structure. The project was begun, and resulted, after a long series of experiments made by various architects, in the splendid edifice which is now regarded by the world as the chief glory of modern Rome. The work made slight progress until the epoch of Julius II., who resumed the great task, and found in Branante an architect capable of comprehending and executing his grandest conceptions. The walls of the ancient Basilica were then wholly removed, and on the 18th day of April, 1508, the foundation-stone of the vast pillars supporting the dome, as we now see it, was laid by Julius with great pomp and ceremony; from that period the work, though carried on with ardor and perseverance, continued during one hundred years to occupy the attention and absorb much of the incomes of eighteen pontiffs. The most celebrated architects of the times displayed their talents in its erection, viz., Bramante, Raphael, San Gillo, Michael Angelo, Vignola, Carlo Maderno, and last, though not least, Bernini, who gave it the final finishing touches of ornamentation, and who built the inclosing colonnade. It is estimated that its cost, after completion, was no less than twelve million pounds sterling,—a sum representing far greater value then than it does in our age. The proportions are as follows: length, seven hundred feet; transept, five hundred feet; height, four hundred and forty feet; breadth of nave, ninety feet; height of nave, one hundred and fifty-four feet. Eustace says, " Entering the piazza, the visitor views four rows of lofty pillars sweeping off to the right and left in bold semicircles. In the centre of the area formed by this immense colonnade an Egyptian obelisk of one solid piece of granite ascends to the height of one hundred and thirty feet; two perpetual fountains, one on each side, play in the air and fall in sheets round the basins of porphyry that receive them. Raised on three successive flights of marble steps, extending four hundred feet in length, and towering to the elevation of one hundred and eighty feet, you see the majestic front of the Basilica itself; this mount is supported by a single row of Corinthian pillars and pilasters, and adorned with an attic, a balustrade, and thirteen colossal statues; far behind and above it rises the matchless dome; two lesser cupolas, one on each side, add not a little to the majesty of the principal dome. Five lofty portals open into the vestibule, four hundred feet in length, seventy feet in height, and fifty in breadth, paved with variegated marble, covered with a gilt vault, adorned with pillars, pilasters, mosaic and bas-reliefs, and terminated at both ends by equestrian statues, one of Constantine, and the other of Charlemagne. Opposite the five portals of the vestibules are the five doors of the church; three are adorned with pillars of the finest marble; that in the centre has panels of bronze.

"Enter; its grandeur overwhelms thee not. The most extensive hall ever constructed by human art expands in magnificence before you. Advancing up the nave you admire the beauty of the variegated marble under your feet and the splendor of the golden vault overhead, the lofty Corinthian pilasters with their bold entablature, the intermediate niches with their statues, the arcades with the graceful figures that recline on the curves of their arches. When you reach the foot of the altar, and, standing in the centre of the church, contemplate the four superb vistas that open around you, and then raise your eyes to the dome at the prodigious elevation of four hundred feet, extending like a firmament over your head and presenting in glowing mosaic the companies of the just and the choirs of celestial spirits, it is sublime; around the dome rise four other cupolas, small indeed when compared to its stupendous magnitude, but of great boldness when considered separately; six more, three on either side, cover the different divisions of the aisles, and six more of greater dimensions canopy as many chapels. All these inferior cupolas are, like the grand dome itself, lined with mosaics; many, indeed, of the masterpieces of paintings which formerly graced this edifice have been removed and replaced by mosaics, which retain all the tints and beauties of the original impressed on a more solid and durable substance. The aisles and altars are adorned with numberless antique pillars, that border the churches all around and form a secondary order; the variegated walls are in many places ornamented with festoons, wreaths, crosses, and medallions representing the effigies of different pontiffs.

"Various monuments rise in different parts of the church, of exquisite sculpture, and form very conspicuous features in the ornamentation of this grand temple. Below the steps of the altar, and of course some distance from it, at the corners on four massive pedestals, four twisted pillars fifty feet in height rise and support an entablature which bears the canopy itself, topped with a cross. The canopy is one hundred and thirty feet from the pavement. This brazen edifice, for so it may be called, was constructed of bronze stripped from the dome of the Pantheon, and is so disposed as not to obstruct the view by concealing the chancel and veiling the chair of Saint Peter. This ornament is also of bronze, and consists of a group of four gigantic figures, representing the four principal doctors of the Greek and Latin churches, supporting the chair at an elevation of seventy feet.

"Under the high altar of Saint Peter's is the tomb of that Apostle, the descent to which is in front, where a large open space leaves room for a double flight of steps. The rails that surround this space above are adorned with one hundred and twelve bronze cornucopiæ, which support as many silver lamps, burning perpetually in honor of the Apostle. Upon the pavement of the small area inclosed by the balustrade is the kneeling statue of Pius VI., by Canova."

The sacristy is connected with Saint Peter's by a long gallery, and is adorned with pillars, statues, paintings, and mosaics. Orders must be obtained here, of Monsignor the Odoli, for visiting the crypt and the dome, which is only open without an order on Thursdays, between eight and ten A.M. Orders for the mosaic manufactory to be obtained from the Rev. Fabricca.

The crypt contains the tombs of the early popes, and also some old bas-reliefs and some very ancient statues of Saint Peter. Adrian IV., the only English pope, is buried here, and also the several distinguished historical characters, including the last of the Stuarts, to whom there is a monument erected in the church, by order of George IV., and executed by Canova; immediately opposite is one to Maria Clementina Sobieski, through which is the entrance to the dome, by a winding path.

On the platform of the roof the cupolas, domes, and pinnacles are seen to advantage, and hence by different staircases, between the walls of the cupola, the hall is reached. During the ascent a fine view may be obtained of the lower parts of the church, as well as of the mosaics and stuccoes which embellish the interior of the dome. On reaching the summit a panoramic view of Rome and the Campagna is had, quite repaying the labor of the ascent.

THE COLOSSEUM.

This vast amphitheatre was erected in the centre of ancient Rome by Vespasian and Titus, from whom it derived its name of the Flavian Amphitheatre. At the present day there remains scarcely anything of what formerly indicated the design of the building; but a small portion of the immense outer shell, which originally both adorned and formed an impenetrable girdle round the whole, has been preserved. In the interior only the brickwork constructions, which have, as it were, grown together with the inclosing wall, are in a state of partial preservation. Vast as the building is, its construction is easily understood, a simple segment of the whole serving to show how all the others succeed one another, like the cells of a beehive. The numerous holes in the stone were made for the purpose of extracting the iron clamps that held the stones together. The external circumference is one thousand nine hundred feet, the long diameter six hundred and fifty-eight feet, the shorter five hundred and fifty-eight feet, height two hundred and two feet.

By applying to the custodian the visitor can ascend to the top, from which there is a most magnificent view. The dens for the wild beasts were below the amphitheatre, as also the apparatus by means of which the arena could be laid under water. The emperor's box was immediately over the entrance.

The building was for a long time used as a quarry, from which several of the palaces in Rome were reared. Should the visitor see the ruin under moonlight, or when it is illuminated with Bengal lights, then he will see it in its grandeur, for it will not bear the brightness of day.

The church of St. Clemente is an edifice belonging to the Irish Dominicans, of which order the Rev. Father Maloney is prior. To his instrumentality we are indebted for the discovery of the ancient churches under the present edifice,—for there are three, one above another,—and on some occasions they are illuminated. Father Maloney has written a pamphlet on his discoveries.

CATACOMBS OF ST. CALIXTUS.

Eighty of Cook & Son's party went into the Catacombs, anciently the quarries made by the Romans for the purpose of extracting the tufa stone or building material. It has long been handed down by priestly tradition that these subterranean passages served as a refuge for the first Christians when persecuted by the emperors; but some antiquarians of the present day hold that neither did the Christians dig them, as asserted, nor did they hide or dwell in them, as they could have no occasion for so doing, these Catacombs being as well known in that age as in this. They are visited by tourists as Christian relics. The guide will be found at the door, who will conduct the visitor through, and explain the Catacombs, finding lights: fee, one franc.

These Catacombs run under the earth for sixty miles. It is estimated that two hundred thousand of the then new sect of Christians were buried here, including foreign popes. A little farther on we wind down a rough road, on the left, leading to the site of what is now occupied by the Church of Saint Urbano. It is built of brick, and the vestibule is supported by marble pillars; the basin in the vestibule—containing the holy water—was found during an excavation; is supposed to be the altar consecrated to Bacchus. At the foot of this hill is the valley of Caffarella. Mr. Wood took us everywhere in Rome to see different objects.

PISA.

We now leave Rome for Pisa, passing through Civita Vecchia and Leghorn. The population of Pisa is fifty-five thousand. The Cathedral is a magnificent structure of white and colored marble, ornamented with relievos, columns, inscriptions, handsome doors, gorgeous roof, a remarkable pulpit, and carved stalls of great beauty in the choir; there are several pictures of great interest.

Another building of interest in Pisa is the Baptistery, begun in 1153. It is a beautiful building, circular in shape, and built entirely of marble. The interior is plain. It contains a fine pulpit, by Nicolo Pisans.

The echo in the Baptistery is marvelously beautiful. The attendant will sound four notes, and the result is a glorious burst of harmony, which, while it is dying away, he will reawaken, and the two echo-choruses will be heard: it is worth going to Pisa to hear.

The Leaning Tower is, as everybody knows, one of the wonders of the world. It was built in 1174, by Bonanno, of Pisa; is one hundred and eighty feet high, and thirteen feet out of perpendicular. Sismondi compares the tower to the usual pictorial representations in children's books of the Tower of Babel. It is a happy simile, and conveys a better idea of the building than chapters of labored descriptions. Nothing can exceed the grace and lightness of the structure; nothing can be more remarkable than its general appearance. In the course of the ascent to its top (which is by an easy staircase) the inclination is very apparent, but at the summit it becomes more so, and gives one the sensation of being in a ship which has keeled over through the action of an ebb-tide. This effect upon the low side, so to speak,—looking over from the gallery and seeing the shaft recede to its base, —is very startling; and I saw a nervous traveler hold on to the tower involuntarily, after glancing down, as if he had some idea of propping it up. The view within from the ground, looking up as through a slanted tube, is also very curious; it certainly inclines as much as the most sanguine tourist could desire. The natural impulse of ninety-nine people out of a hundred who were about to recline upon the grass below it to rest, and contemplate the adjacent buildings, would probably be not to take up their position on the leaning side, it is so very slant. Fee to ascend the tower, one-half to one franc, not fewer than three in a party.

SPEZZIA.

We now make our way for Spezzia. We stopped at the Hôtel De la Ville. This was the first day the hotel was opened. It was new, and one of the most perfect hotels I was ever in, being built in the finest style.

Spezzia stands at the head of the gulf of the same name, in a beautiful situation, between two fortified ranges of rock. It is a favorite bathing and boating place, and the environs are delightful—notably Porto Venere. Its most remarkable structures are the old citadel and the ancient castle of the Visconti. In the bay may be seen the strange appearance called Palla, a hemispherical swell of the sea, caused by a submarine spring of fresh water. The diameter of the Palla is twenty-five feet.

Mr. Marsh, a Baptist minister, bought property at Spezzia, and has a school of one hundred and fifty scholars. They do not teach English, but Arabic.

We now start for Genoa. Before we got out of the city some person threw a stone into the car in which five persons besides myself were seated. It broke one of the large lights into a hundred pieces. One piece went into a gentleman's eye, and it injured him considerably. I don't see how we escaped as well as we did.

There are fifty-five tunnels from Spezzia to Genoa. One tunnel runs under Genoa for one and a half miles. The whole distance is about one hundred and five miles, and we traveled under ground seventy miles.

GENOA.

The position of the city and port of Genoa is one of the finest and loveliest in the world. It is a splendid amphitheatre, terrace rising above terrace, garden upon garden, palace upon palace, height upon height. Its beauty has been compared with that of Bath, Naples, and Constantinople. Genoa was known to the Romans, and some traces of the Roman walls are yet to be found; though since the first circuit of walls was built the included space has been greatly enlarged, so that at the present time the inner walls comprise a circuit of seven miles, and the broad compart of the outer walls is no less than twenty miles in circumference.

The magnificent harbor of Genoa was the cause of the mediæval prosperity of the city. The republic was founded in the tenth century, and long rivaled Pisa and Venice. The head of the republic was called the Doge, and was generally elected from the four great families of Genoa, the Doria, Spinola, Grimaldi, and the Fieschi. The two former were Ghibellines, the two latter Guelphs; and these party divisions in Genoa, as in other

Italian cities, were the frequent causes of fierce domestic struggles.

In the sixteenth century a new constitution was given to the Genoese by Andrea Doria, but the power of the city was then declining. Her rich possessions in the Levant gradually fell into the hands of the Turks, her trade diminished, and her wealth lessened. Genoa was subsequently attacked by the French and Germans. In 1805 it was annexed to the French Empire, and in 1815 was ceded to Sardinia. It is now one of the most flourishing Italian ports. Commerce is returning to Genoa, and, with Italian liberty, better and more prosperous times seem to be in store for her.

The Genoese have borne but an indifferent character, though the Tuscan proverb is an exaggeration which says, "Genoa has a sea without fish, mountains without trees, men without faith, and women without virtue."

The harbor is about two miles in diameter, and is protected by two moles. That to the east is called the Molo Vecchio (old mole); the western mole is the Molo Nuovo (new mole). The opening of the harbor between the extreme points of the moles is about the third of a mile wide. At the extremity of each mole is a light, and on a tongue of land to the south of the new mole is a new lighthouse, the lantern of which is five hundred and twenty feet above the level of the sea.

The interior of the lighthouse, which stands on a hill of considerable elevation, may be visited, and from the top (fee for admission, fifty cents) a magnificent prospect of open sea, harbor, and city is obtained. The railway skirts the harbor, and tramways are laid down on many of the quays.

The Arsenal and Royal Dock-yards are to the north of the harbor. The Custom House was formerly the Bank of Saint George, the most ancient banking establishment in Europe. It was founded in 1346, and continued to exist until the French Revolution. In writing of the foundation of the Bank of England, Macaulay says: "The Bank of Saint George had nearly completed its third century; it had begun to receive deposits and to make loans before Columbus had crossed the Atlantic, before Gama had twined the Cape, when a Christian Emperor was reigning at Constantinople, when a Mahommedan Sultan was reigning at Grenada, when Florence was a Republic, and when Holland obeyed a hereditary Prince. All these things had been changed. The Turk was at Constantinople, the Castilian was at Grenada, Florence had its hereditary Prince, but the Bank of Saint George was still receiving deposits and making loans."

Why should not the Bank of London be as great and as durable as the Bank of Genoa? The English traveler who is detained by vexatious custom-house regulations in this fine old building, may perhaps remember the proverb, "As safe as the Bank of England."

Genoa is pre-eminently the city of palaces. It is impossible to describe the endless details of those rich palaces, the walls of some of them within alive with masterpieces of Vandyck; the great heavy stone balconies, one above another, and tier over tier, with here and there one larger than the rest, towering high up, a huge marble platform; the doorless vestibules, massively buried windows, immense public staircases, thick marble pillars, strong, dungeon-like arches, and dreary, dreaming, echoing, vaulted chambers, among which the eye wanders again and again, as every palace is succeeded by another; the terrace gardens between house and house, with green arches of the pine, and groves of orange-trees, and blushing oleander in full bloom, twenty, thirty, forty feet above the street; the painted halls mouldering and rotting in the dark corners, and shining out in beautiful colors and voluptuous designs where the walls are dry; the faded figures on the outside of the houses holding wreaths and crowns, and flying upward and downward, and standing in niches, and here and there looking fainter and more feeble than elsewhere by contrast with some fresh little Cupids, who, on a more recently decorated portion of the front, are stretching out what seems to be the semblance of a blanket, but is indeed a sun-dial; and the steep, up-hill streets of small palaces looking down on close by-ways.

The Doria palace was remodeled by Andrea Doria, called the father of his country, who died in 1560, at an extreme age. The palace is beautifully situated, its gardens extending to the sea. The walks are laid out with cypress- and orange-trees, and are adorned with choice vases and statues. The reliefs and general decoration of the palace were designed by Pierino del Vaga, pupil of Raphael. The principal rooms shown are the great hall, corridor, containing the family portraits, and the saloon. In the garden is a monument to a favorite dog which belonged to Andrea Doria.

Genoa has one hundred and five churches of different denominations.

STATUE OF COLUMBUS.

The statue of Columbus is near the railway station. Columbus was born at Cogoleto, a small town on the Rivera di Pouenti, along which the road to Nice passes; the monument is of white marble, and is surrounded with sitting figures, representing Religion, Wisdom, Force, and Geography. Between these are reliefs, the subjects of which are taken from the history of Columbus. The statue at the top represents the discoverer; it rests on an anchor, and a figure of America kneels at its feet. Near the statue is the palace of Columbus, with an inscription. There is a small statue to him in a street near the harbor.

There are hundreds of things I could mention about Genoa, but I will stop.

MILAN.

We now make our way to Milan, the capital of Lombardy, and one of the most thriving cities of Italy, ranking second as regards population. Travelers coming to Italy by any of the Alpine passes from Switzerland—the Simplon, the St. Gotthard, or the Splugen—are here introduced into life, the city being the terminus of those three great routes. The population is over two hundred and twelve thousand, exclusive of soldiers, and the circumference of the city, which in shape resembles a hexagon, is about eight miles; the average height above the level of the sea is four hundred and thirty English feet; it is watered by the little river Oloud, a tributary of the Po.

MILAN CATHEDRAL.

Milan Cathedral is the largest Gothic church in the world; it covers an area of nearly one hundred and eight thousand square feet, a space nearly twice that occupied by the cathedral of Canterbury. Its form is that of a Latin cross. The dimensions of the building are as follows: extreme length, four hundred and eighty-six feet; breadth, two hundred and fifty-two feet; length, two hundred and eighty-eight feet; width of nave, exclusive of four aisles, sixty-three feet; height of naves from the pavement to the statue of the Virgin on the spire, three hundred and fifty-five feet, and from the pavement to crown of the vaulting, one hundred and fifty-five feet.

The best view of the cathedral is from the plaza facing the church; this plaza has been greatly enlarged and improved by the removal of several buildings which obstructed the view, and is now a very handsome square.

TURIN.

We now make our way to Turin, population, two hundred and twelve thousand, one of the most flourishing Italian cities; at the same time it is one of the least interesting, as it contains few monuments of antiquity, and, as compared with many smaller places, has fewer works of art or magnificent churches or palaces. It is, however, by no means to be neglected by the traveler, who will probably be here introduced to Italian scenes and Italian life.

The city, which is exceedingly well laid out, with fine wide streets, some of them of considerable length, is situated on a plain between the river Po and the Dora Raparan, at about eight hundred and twenty feet above the level of the sea; it derives its name from the Taurini, a Ligurian tribe, who were attacked and defeated by Hannibal, B.C. 218; subsequently a Roman city called Augusta Taurinorum occupied part of the site of Turin.

Of this city there are no architectural remains, the amphitheatre and their ruins having been destroyed by Francis I. in 1536. Since then, however, it has stood several sieges. In 1706, after having been heroically defended against the French, who did much injury to the fortifications and buildings, the siege was raised after a battle in which the French were signally defeated by the imperial army under Prince Eugene.

Turin was the capital of the kingdom of Sardinia until 1859, when it became the capital of Italy. In 1864, however, the capital was removed to Florence, and in 1874 to Rome. Since the removal of the court and parliament Turin has somewhat declined in importance, although, as already stated, it is still a flourishing place.

There are three railway stations at Turin. The Central Station (Stazione Centrale) is the terminus of all the lines; the other stations are the Stazione Porta-Luca and the Stazione Succursale, on the left bank of the Dora.

There are more than forty churches in Turin, but only a few demand the visitor's special attention. The cathedral (Duomo) is the oldest church; the present building was begun in 1498, and was consecrated seven years after. The west front is of marble; in the interior are several modern frescoes, that over the western door being a copy of the Last Supper by Leonardo da Vinci; the roof contains representations of events in early scriptural history, and over the arches are incidents from the life of Saint John the Baptist. Turin is not far from the Alps.

MONT CENIS TUNNEL.

We now make our way to Mont Cenis tunnel. As early as 1857 experiments were undertaken before a government commission to see if the idea of a tunnel through the Alps, which had long occupied the minds of engineers in France and Italy, was practicable. A machine was invented which should be worked by means of highly-compressed air, and after this compressed air had performed its duty should be made available as a source of ventilation. As soon as this machine was tested and found to work, bridges, roads, and houses were constructed, and in November, 1860, five compressors were at work. But it was not until 1863 that the work went successfully ahead; up to that time the machinery was found to do little more than could be accomplished by manual labor; but in that year great improvements were made in the machinery, and wonderful progress was effected, so that in 1870 the work was completed.

The history of the schemes, the description of the machinery constructed by Sommeiller, Grandis, and Gratoni, the failures and successes, have been so often told that it will be only necessary here to say that the tunnel is from seven to eight miles long, and the passage occupies sixty-five minutes; it is twenty-six feet wide and nineteen feet high, and is built up with good walls of masonry throughout; it rises from the north (three thousand nine hundred and four feet above the sea) by a gradient of two in ninety-one to its highest point, four thousand three hundred and seventy-seven feet, or three thousand four hundred and eighty feet below the Alps overhead; it then descends by a slope of one in two hundred to its south opening, near Bardonneche. On the Italian side it is four thousand three hundred feet above the sea.

Mont Cenis is not a suitable name for the tunnel, as that Alpine height is fully sixteen miles away from any point of it. The actual mountains under which the tunnel passes are the Col de Frejus, the Grand Vallon (the highest), and the Col de la Rue.

One of the most wonderful things in connection with the tunnel is that there is no vertical shaft. It could therefore only be worked from the two mouths towards the centre, and it could not have been worked at all if machinery had not been invented which should bore the tunnel and supply air at the same time.

There is nothing disagreeable in the passage; the air is not closer or more unpleasant than in the underground railway in London. The carriages are all well lighted, and the tunnel itself is lighted at convenient distances throughout.

Emerging from the tunnel, the scene, at whatever time of the year, is very striking; when the snow is upon the ground and the sun is shining the blaze of light is dazzling, so much so as to be positively painful, and the scene around is wild and lonely, almost savage. In the summer the prospect is singularly beautiful, and at all times the sensation of traveling by rail at that great height is pleasant from its novelty.

Every mile of the journey to Bardonneche until the train reaches the level land in the valley of France is full of interest, and many of the views obtained are of exquisite beauty. Following the course of the torrent of Bardonneche, the beautiful valley of the Dora Riparia is reached, and, although there are fifty tunnels, the views obtained at intervals are exquisite: the wild and romantic gorge, the peaks and passes of surrounding mountains, curious little villages nestling beside great rocks, and all around vegetation of rich growth and fruitfulness.

PARIS.

We passed a great many villages in France before we reached Paris. We arrived here at 9 A.M. and put up at the Grand Hotel, situated on the Boulevard des Capucines, opposite the termination of the Rue de la Paix, which leads to the Tuileries. As the stranger is unquestionably desirous to "do" Paris, the first city of the world, we will immediately proceed to describe the centre, where magnificence, elegance, and luxury reign supreme. The Grand Hotel joins the new Opera-House, in close proximity to the leading theatres and principal railway stations, and the very centre of the life and gayety of modern Paris. This magnificent structure was built by the same company that own the Hôtel du Louvre, and in the same elegant style as that world-renowned establishment; it is entirely isolated from all other buildings, and covers an extent of nine thousand square yards (about the same as the Louvre). It has a frontage on the boulevards of three hundred and ninety feet. Its different façades contain four hundred and forty-four windows in addition to those in the court-yards, ground-floor, and entresol. The rooms number seven hundred, nearly all of which are furnished in the most luxuriant style. Its dining-room is the most magnificent in the world. Leading from its beautiful court of honor are reading-rooms, cafés, billiard saloon, reception room, telegraph office, etc. Under the new and admirable direction of Mr. Vanhymbeeck, an American, the charge for service has been suppressed, and rooms can be had at fixed prices; the best rooms, including breakfast and dinner with wines, six dollars per day, next best five dollars per day, and next best four dollars per day. The situation of the Hôtel du Louvre is delightful, and the amusements about the house so varied that it is almost unnecessary to go out to look for any other; it occupies a whole block, covering about two acres of ground, and is bounded by Rue Rivoli in the front, Rue St. Honore in the rear, and Place du Palais Royal and Rue de Marengo on the other two sides. It was built by a stock company, and is conducted on the same plan as our hotels, with the exception that you breakfast and dine out, paying only for your rooms, the prices varying from twenty francs to six dollars, according to the floor you are on, and whether you are on the inside or outside of the court. From the court a magnificent double staircase leads to a Corinthian gallery, occupied as a reading-room. Here you will find all the leading papers, magazines, and reviews. This beautiful saloon with us would be called the public parlor and conversation room. Here the ladies and gentlemen, guests of the house, meet, read the news, and discuss the topics of the day. This saloon communicates with a spacious dining hall and two small breakfast and tea rooms. Each room has its own office, service, and waiters. Your bills are sent weekly to your rooms, and you pay them at the general office in the court. There need never be any mistakes in your bill, unless it is your own fault, as the custom is to write on a card for everything you want; always do that, and never pay but for what your card calls. In every room in the house you will find the regulations, with the price of that particular room and for service; that with the card you give must be your bill. The house is owned by the Credit Mobilier, and conducted by M. Montague as principal director, a gentleman in whom information, politeness, and unremitting attention to the wants of his guests are happily blended.

RESTAURANTS AND CAFÉS.

The best of these are the Trois Frères Provençaux, Café Riche, Anglais, and Voisin's. The cafés, as a general rule, only furnish *déjeuners a la fourchette*, chocolate, coffee, tea, ices, and liquors. The restaurants Voisin and Riche are considered by epicures to have the best cooks in Paris, and Americans, when giving breakfast- or dinner-parties, generally prefer those, being not only the best but the most economical.

The cafés are institutions almost peculiar to Paris, having existed here for over a century and a half. They are among the most remarkable features of the French capital. They are to be found in every quarter of the city, and are generally decorated with much taste and splendor. Those most brilliantly ornamented are situated on the Boulevard Poissonnière, Boulevard des Italians, Boulevard Montmartre, Boulevard de Capucines, and Boulevard le Madéleine. When lighted up at night they present a scene of enchantment difficult to describe. Here it is that the Frenchman is seen in all his glory, seated near a small table in front of the café, enjoying his coffee, his petit verré, his sugar and water, or his absinthe. Nothing can be more delightful than witnessing this splendid scene. Every seat occupied outside and inside; men, women, and children, all either eating, drinking, smoking, or talking; the blaze of light, the reflection of mirrors, the clinking of glasses, and the hum of conversation must surely amuse the pleasure-seekers.

There are also some very fine cafés on the Boulevard Sévastopol, where, while you are enjoying your cigar, sipping your coffee, drinking your ale or liquor, you are amused by the singing of some of the best vocalists in Paris. There is no charge for admittance into these establishments, but you are expected to call for refreshments of some kind on entering.

The city of Paris is the most splendid city I have ever seen. I have been over America, Cuba, England, Switzerland, Holland, Germany, Austria, Italy, Egypt, the Holy Land, Japan, China, India, and many other places, but I have never seen any city to compare with Paris. The streets are wide, the Voistres and the Boulevard des Capucines being the widest and the best in Paris. There is nothing to be compared with it in any country. There are a great many fountains of different kinds. The houses are very high, more so than in any other city.

CALAIS.

We proceed from Paris to Calais, distant two hundred miles, passing on the way a great many cities. From here we crossed the channel to Dover, and then to London, distant eighty miles.

The following is taken from a daily newspaper (political, literary, artistical, and commercial), published in Aden:

"ROUND THE WORLD.

"The third annual tour round the world, arranged under the auspices of Messrs. Cook & Son, of London, and conducted by Mr. A. G. Caprani, is now of the past. This party reached Cairo all well some two weeks ago, and there the itineraries of many of the tourists lay in different directions, some hurrying to England, the quickest possible way, others to Austria, Germany, Belgium, while others, including Mr. A. G. Caprani, the conductor, had still further excursions to make in the direction of Palestine, Turkey, Greece, etc. It will be remembered this party left London September 5 last year for New York. Their journey included a trip across the great American continent, and they visited Niagara Falls, Detroit, Salt Lake City, Chicago, Sacramento, San Francisco; from thence by the Pacific Company's mail steamer to Yokohama, and on to Hong Kong, visiting various points of interest in China; from thence to Singapore, Penang, Ceylon, and Calcutta, from which point the journey was resumed across the Indian Continent to Bombay, and from thence to Aden, Suez, and Cairo. Among the number of passengers who left Alexandria by the Zambesi, of the P. & O. Co., on the 15th, en route for Brindisi and Venice, were three gentlemen of distinct nationality,—viz., an American, a Belgian, and a German,—who were completing their tour of pleasure around the world, and had traveled with this party, and all speak with admiration of the great tact and energy displayed by Mr. A. G. Caprani, the responsible director of the tour, who seems to have been also their leader, adviser, general paymaster, banker, and companion, conversing alternately and fluently in the three or four idioms spoken among this international party of tourists.

"All are loud in their praises for the liberal and efficient manner in which Messrs. Cook have fulfilled their stipulations. Every expense was covered in their contracts; every member of the party was totally relieved of every care; and, when we think that it is possible for them to visit so many interesting countries, traveling about twenty-five thousand miles without having to pay any hotel bills or experiencing any trouble in looking after their luggage or from other petty annoyances usually inherent with the pleasure of traveling even in

Europe, we do not wonder at their asserting that nobody has ever accomplished such a journey with greater ease and comfort. The conditions of climate, which were most propitious, and the continued fine weather throughout their long ramble of six months, certainly contributed not a little to the success of the trip.

"The party was chiefly composed of young people, except one, an American gentleman, native of Phœnixville, Pennsylvania, who prides himself in the belief that few at his age would venture to follow in his track. Mr. John Vanderslice may almost certainly be said to have been the first who had carried his seventy-four years round the world in such a pleasant and easy manner as he appears to do, and we heartily wish his health may continue good yet for many years to relate to his grandchildren the sights of Japan, China, the tropical regions, India, Egypt, Italy, etc., etc.

" Mr. Thomas Cook, the world-renowned veteran of tours, announces his second tour around the world, starting from England in September next, providing there are twenty depositors, and the itinerary will be to a great extent that taken by the party who have just completed the tour under the charge of our countryman, M. Caprani."

LONDON.

London, the metropolis of the United Kingdom of Great Britain, and the most wealthy city in the world, had a population in 1874 of three million eight hundred and fifty thousand, nearly one million increase in twenty years. The present increase is fifty thousand per annum, or a birth every thirteen minutes. The city covers an extent of one hundred and forty square miles, or fourteen miles long and ten broad; three hundred and eighty thousand houses are occupied by the population, and the cost of food is supposed to be eight hundred thousand dollars per day. Although the climate of London is by no means pleasant, its sanitary advantages over other capitals are remarkable. According to statistics, out of every thousand inhabitants twenty-four die annually in London.

The houses are large and regular, the streets wide and clean, but the sameness of its appearance is rather oppressive; its inhabitants are mostly city merchants and professional men, who live very close to the charming ring of fashion, expecting yearly to take the leap across.

London is of great antiquity. The Romans surrounded it with walls, but nothing is known of it previous to that time. In the time of Nero it bore the dignity of a Roman colony. During the last eight hundred years it has suffered much from fire and pestilence. Its police regulations are admirable, and it is considered to-day one of the best governed cities in the world. London is particularly distinguished by the air of business which pervades its streets, especially in the city. The west has more the air of Paris, St. Petersburg, and other capitals. The streets are mostly wide, clean, and well paved, the houses plain and substantial, the architecture of the clubs and public buildings substantial and elegant. The most fashionable part of London is the West End, and here, as I have said, reside the aristocracy of England (that is, during the season, which lasts from February to August).

I started from Phœnixville, Pennsylvania, September, 1874. By the time I get to New York I will have traveled on the great ocean more than thirty-seven thousand five hundred miles. We have been tossed upon the uneasy sea as a thing of no account; though we always prepared ourselves as well as we could to withstand the blast, we could not keep the deck and were forced to go below. I was lying on the locker one day in the main cabin, when a heaving swell tossed the ship upon her side, throwing the large marble slab of the heater from its fastenings; it struck near me on the floor and was dashed into a dozen pieces. I have traveled over thirty-nine thousand three hundred miles by railroad, stages, and other vehicles. I am now better in health than when I started from Phœnixville. I hope to get to Liverpool and go on the Cunard line across the Atlantic Ocean to New York, Philadelphia, and then home.

The captains, under-officers, and hotel keepers all say I am the oldest man that ever started from New York, Philadelphia, or any other point, to sail on a tour around the world in good health and spirits. I give thanks to the kind Providence which has been over us in all the perils of the land and of the seas, and more thankful than ever shall I be if I get to my home once more. Here evermore may our home be until our journeyings on earth shall come to an end, and we take our departure to a better country in heaven.

I went out this morning to hear Mr. Spurgeon preach at the great Baptist church. I got in, but it was very much crowded; I had to stand two-thirds of the time, then a gentleman gave me a seat. Mr. Spurgeon is one of the best of preachers; the singing was very good; the church holds from ten to twelve thousand persons; there are three galleries, and there were two or three hundred standing. Perhaps this is one of the greatest Baptist churches in the world. I went to get my ticket to take me to Liverpool, and got a ticket for the Celtic, five thousand tons, of the White Star line. I expect to get on the steamer on the 29th day of April, 1875.

LONDON, April 19, 1875.

The following article appeared in the "Independent Phœnix," of Phœnixville, Pa., in October, 1875:

"GOLDEN WEDDING.

"On last Wednesday evening, the 20th instant, we enjoyed the pleasure, with many other invited guests, of meeting under the hospitable roof of Mr. and Mrs. John Vanderslice, in honor of the fiftieth anniversary of the marriage of that worthy couple—their Golden Wedding. It falls to the lot of but few to live together happily in wedlock for a term of fifty years, and it is meet that such an occasion should receive a precious mark. Both—Mr. Vanderslice in his seventy-fifth and Mrs. Vanderslice in her seventy-first year—are in the enjoyment of good health, and on this occasion received the congratulations of their many friends, and entered into the enjoyments of the evening with all the zest and sparkle of youth. The south rooms of the mansion were used as reception-rooms, and there the friends met socially until the season for refreshments, when they were ushered into the north rooms, where all were bountifully refreshed from a table most heavily and artistically laden with all the delicacies of the season, the Rev. Mr. Stenger, pastor, having first asked the blessing of God. The presents for the occasion were arranged on a table in an upper room, and were both numerous and handsome.

Out of regard to the wishes of the friends we will not particularize in this respect.

"After doing ample justice to the good things provided, the party again assembled in the south rooms, and J. B. Morgan, Esq., our worthy burgess, treated those present to a brief genealogical record of the family, after which L. B. Kaler introduced Rev. William Smith, of Plymouth Meeting (Baptist), Montgomery County, who spoke feelingly of the long life of usefulness and prosperity passed together by Mr. and Mrs. Vanderslice,— Mr. Smith as pastor of the Phœnixville Church having baptized and received them into the church some forty-one years ago.

"John Vanderslice is the son of John and Deborah Vanderslice, of East Pikeland Township, and was born May 27, 1801. Mrs. Vanderslice is the daughter of Nicholas and Christiana Custer, of Vincent, and was born February 14, 1805. They were married October 20, 1825, and started in life with nothing in the way of worldly possessions. He, for the first four years of his married life, worked his father's farm on shares, then spent two years at butchering, when he bought a farm at Kimberton for three thousand dollars, which he lived upon for seven years, greatly improved it, and sold it for nine thousand dollars. Then, in the year 1840, he bought a farm of sixty-five acres, at eighty dollars per acre, in what is now known as the North Ward of this borough; the old homestead on the site of the present mansion was torn down, and the present one erected. About that time there were about a dozen houses on the north side of the creek. In 1842 he laid out his farm in town lots, and in the next three years sold many lots, and saw a town growing up around him. For many acres he realized three thousand dollars per acre, thus making a very profitable real estate speculation. Nine children were born to them,— five sons and four daughters; a son and a daughter died in infancy; the remaining sons and daughters, with some twenty-two grandchildren, graced the golden wedding.

"Mr. Vanderslice has also won quite a reputation as a traveler, having visited London and Paris no less than five times, Italy and Rome three times, and bears the honor of being the only man, so far as known, who carried his seventy-four years in a voyage around the world with all the vigor and earnestness of youth. He left his home here on the 28th of September, 1874, and went by rail to San Francisco, thence across the Pacific to China, down the Red Sea to Egypt, and then took the course for home. Our readers will remember the interesting letters of travel from his pen that we published during the eight months of his pilgrimage.

"But, to return to our subject of the Golden

Wedding, rarely has it been our lot to be present at so social and happy a gathering, and we know that such must be the feeling of all who tendered heartfelt congratulations to Mr. and Mrs. John Vanderslice on this semi-centennial anniversary."

The following extracts are from "The Keystone," Philadelphia, Saturday, March 27, 1875:

"FUNERAL OF BROTHER A. F. SHANAFELT.

"On Monday afternoon, March 22, the remains of Brother Rev. A. F. Shanafelt, pastor of the First Baptist Church, Chester, Pennsylvania, were committed to their last resting-place, in the Chester rural cemetery, with impressive Masonic ceremonies. The religious service occurred in the Baptist church, where some twenty clergymen of different denominations, and a vast audience of the friends of the deceased, including the brethren of Chester and L. H. Scott Lodges and members of Saint John's Commandery of this city, were present to pay honor to the memory of the deceased.

"Feeling addresses were delivered by a number of the clergy, after which the remains of our muchloved brother were viewed by some fifteen hundred persons, which demonstrated the affectionate regard in which Brother Shanafelt was held by the entire community of Chester. The Masonic services at the grave were, by request, conducted by Brother Edward Masson, acting W. M., whose impassioned address was an earnest tribute to the Masonic virtues of one who, in his daily life, illustrated the loftiest tenets of Freemasonry. Brother Shanafelt has passed to the higher life, where, no one can doubt, he has received an abundant entrance into the Grand Lodge above."

"DEATH OF AN AGED MASON AND PRINTER.

"The oldest printer in Pennsylvania, Brother John H. Royer, died very suddenly at his residence in Phœnixville, Pa., on Wednesday evening, the 17th inst. That day he must have had a premonition of his approaching end, as he had a long talk with his wife in reference to his death and as to who should speak at his funeral, naming the Revs. H. S. Miller and Brother M. Rowland, the disposition of his body,—that it should be buried in Morris Cemetery, and that the Masonic Fraternity should have charge of the ceremonies. He was upon the street the last day of his life, in his usual good state of health.

"Brother John H. Royer was born near Hobson's School-house, Montgomery County, Pa., on the 22d of February, 1793. He served his apprenticeship at the 'Register' office in Norristown, commencing in the year 1812. During his apprenticeship the war of that year broke out, and he was among the first to enlist under the banner of his country. At the conclusion of that conflict he returned to Norristown and finished his apprenticeship. At the expiration of his time he went to Washington, where he worked as a journeyman.

"In 1819 he started the 'Pottstown Times,' which he successfully conducted for a number of years, and which afterwards became the 'Montgomery Ledger,' which is now a large and flourishing paper; subsequently he printed a daily paper, in Philadelphia, about the time the 'Public Ledger' was started. He was the projector of the first English paper published in Lehigh County, the 'Lehigh Bulletin,' which made its appearance in 1837. This paper he conducted for twelve years, and then sold it, when its name was changed to the 'Allentown Democrat,' which it still bears. Later he published the 'West Philadelphia Record' and also 'The Banner.' In 1857 he went to Phœnixville, and in April of that year issued the first number of the 'Weekly Phœnix,' now the 'Independent Phœnix,' which was conducted by Brothers Royer & Son. About three years ago he retired from active business, and settled down to the quieter walks and enjoyments of life, but he still retained his passionate liking for the printer's case, and frequently would he do a fair day's work in the office of the 'Spring City Sun' (published by his son, Brother John H. Royer), either at the press or before the case. One of these feats of skill he accomplished one week before his death, which was the printing of four thousand envelopes and one thousand tags, for a leading firm in Spring City, a thousand of which envelopes were printed in the space of one hour. The setting up one thousand ems in one hour, quite a feat for one so aged, he took a modest pride in exhibiting.

"The funeral of Brother Royer took place on Sunday, the 21st inst., and was participated in by the Masonic Fraternity and the military of the town. Phœnix Lodge, No. 75, A. Y. M., had charge of the funeral, the brethren turning out in large numbers. The military of the place, including the Griffin Battery, the Reeves Rifles, the Emmet Guards, and the Wheatley Cadets, were also out in full force, headed by the Phœnixville Military Band, all under the command of F. A. Tencate. Major-General J. R. Dobson and staff were also present, and led the procession to the church and cemetery. Services were held in the Baptist Church, conducted by Brother Maxwell Rowland and the Rev. H. S. Miller. The sermon delivered by Brother Rowland was able and eloquent, and was listened to with marked attention. The singing was very fine, being led by Brother John O. K. Robarts, editor of the 'Phœnixville Messenger.' At the grave, Phœnix Lodge, No. 75, performed the last sad Masonic rites, Brother P. M. Levi B. Kaler officiating as W. M. The funeral was one of the largest the town ever witnessed, and showed in what esteem the deceased brother was held.

"Brother Royer was made a Mason in 1820, and was, therefore, not only the oldest printer in the State, but also one of the oldest Masons."

I received two letters in London, April 12, 1875, from Cook & Sons' chief office, Ludgate Circuit, London, one containing the notice of the death of A. F. Shanafelt, pastor of the First Baptist Church, Chester, Pa., and the other the death of an aged Mason and printer, the oldest printer in Pennsylvania, Brother John H. Royer, who died at his residence in Phœnixville, Pa.

JOHN VANDERSLICE.

INDEX.

	PAGE
Aden	262
Agra and Taj	246
Airolo	17
Alexandria	103, 270
Alps	18
Altorf	19
Amsterdam	28
Ancient Cemetery in Japan	178
Animal Food in China	199
Antwerp	36
Army	60, 61, 63
Arnheim	28
Ayr	43
Babylon	112
Baden-Baden	23, 81
Ballymena	54
Basle	21
Belfast	53
Benares	243
Bengal	225
Berlin	85
Bethany	126
Bethlehem	123
Beyrout	138
Bombay	260
Born	9
Brahmins	241
Brindisi	271
Brussels	36
Butchering	10
Cairo	106, 267
Calais	311
Calcutta	233

	PAGE
California	67
California Fruits and Grain	161
Campo Santo Vecchio, Naples	283
Canton	194
Cawnpoor	252
Ceylon	228
Charlestown	9
Chicago	56, 142
Chinese Temples in San Francisco	160
Chinese Theatre in San Francisco	158
Coblentz	25
Coleraine	54, 55
Cologne	26, 83
"Colorado" Steamer	167
Columbus, Statue of, in Genoa	300
Convent	125
Council Bluffs	146
Crimes in Japan	182
Cuba	57
Damascus	136
Dayton	9
Dead Sea	125
Delhi	255
Detroit	59
Devil's Ink	140
Disposal of the Dead in Japan	183
Dresden	87
Dusseldorf	27, 84

	PAGE		PAGE
Edinburgh	47, 70	Lucerne	20
Farm	10	Madras	227
Farming	9	Married	9
Florence	14	Marseilles	11
Fort Sumter	65	Mayence	25
Frankfort	24	McGregor's	58
Galveston	66	Milan	16, 301
Gambling in China	202	Mobile	58
Ganges, the	242	Mont Cenis Tunnel	304
Geneva	79	Munich	90
Geneva Lake	80	Nabulus	128
Genoa	296	Nagasaki	189
Gettysburg	62	Naples	12, 100, 273
Giant's Causeway	54	Nazareth	130
Glasgow	44, 68	New Orleans	57, 66
Golden Wedding	316	Nutmeg Grove in Singapore	220
Greenock	52	Oban	52
Haarlem	31	Omaha	146
Hague	34	Opium	239
Hanover	85	Pacific, on the	167
Heidelberg	23	Paisley	43
Herculaneum	277	Paris	11, 38, 77, 306
Hong Kong	193	Penang	224
India, Natives of	239	Pensacola	66
Indiana	10	Perth	50
Inland Sea of Japan	187	Phœnixville	10
Innspruck	91	Pisa	12, 13, 293
Jacksonville	65	Pompeii	12, 278
Jacob's Well	129	Portland	59
Japan and the Japanese	180	Port Said	114
Japan, excursions in	172	Prague	88
Japanese habits	186	Pyramids	112
"Japan" Steamer, Wreck of	203	Quebec	59
Jericho	126	Rachel's Tomb	123
Jerusalem	121	Ramleh	120
Joppa or Jaffa	114	Red Sea	263
Jordan	126	Religions of China	202
Kehr Hauwar	136	Religions of the Japanese	183
Kussert	63	Rome	13, 96, 284
Leipsic	86	Rotterdam	34
Leyden	33	Royer, John H	320
Lisburn	54	Safed	134
Liverpool	56, 71	Salt Lake	153
London	11, 39, 72, 313	San Francisco	153
		Shanafelt, A. F., Funeral of	319

INDEX.

	PAGE		PAGE
Shanghai	190	Taverns	13
Sherman	148	Tea	200
Silk-weaving	197	Tiberias	131
Singapore	219	Tonsure, the, in Japan	185
Small Feet of Chinese Women	200	"Tourist," the	140
		Turin	302
Snakes in India	259	Typhoons	196
Solomon's Pools	123	Tyre—Hiram	139
Spezzia	295	Venice	15, 92
Stirling Castle	50	Verona	16
Stirling	51	Vesuvius	276
St. Louis	57	Vienna	89
St. Paul	59	Washington	58, 64
Strasbourg	21, 80	Wesel	27
Suez	113, 267	Yeddo	177
Tallahassee	66	Yokohama	174

THE END.